Lecture Notes in Artificial Intelligence 10096

Subseries of Lecture Notes in Computer Science

More information about this series at http://www.springer.com/series/1244

David Riaño · Richard Lenz
Manfred Reichert (Eds.)

Knowledge Representation
for Health Care

HEC 2016 International Joint Workshop, KR4HC/ProHealth 2016
Munich, Germany, September 2, 2016
Revised Selected Papers

Springer

Editors
David Riaño
Universitat Rovira i Virgili
Tarragona
Spain

Manfred Reichert
University of Ulm
Ulm
Germany

Richard Lenz
University of Erlangen and Nuremberg
Erlangen
Germany

ISSN 0302-9743   ISSN 1611-3349   (electronic)
Lecture Notes in Artificial Intelligence
ISBN 978-3-319-55013-8   ISBN 978-3-319-55014-5   (eBook)
DOI 10.1007/978-3-319-55014-5

Library of Congress Control Number: 2017933276

LNCS Sublibrary: SL7 – Artificial Intelligence

Printed on acid-free paper

This Springer imprint is published by Springer Nature
The registered company is Springer International Publishing AG
The registered company address is: Gewerbestrasse 11, 6330 Cham, Switzerland

Preface

The introduction of computers in health care can contribute toward homogenizing services, increase the quality of those services, and reduce the costs of health-care systems. Two of the computer-based approaches to provide these benefits are supported on technologies for knowledge representation and process-oriented management. These technologies include medical data analysis and processing, clinical practice modeling, intelligent decision support systems and recommenders, clinical process management, personalized and patient-centric e-Health and m-Health, etc.

The Joint International Workshop KR4HC-ProHealth represents the effort of two communities to bring together experts in these technologies in order to present new advances and to deliver results on promising intelligent systems and technologies supporting clinical tasks. Two are the main viewpoints that converge in the workshop:

- As part of medical informatics, the knowledge-representation for health care (KR4HC) view focuses on representing and reasoning with medical knowledge in computers as a means to support knowledge management and clinical decision-making. This community aims at developing efficient representations, technologies, and tools for integrating all the important elements that health-care providers work with: electronic medical records (EMRs) and health-care information systems, clinical practice guidelines, and standardized medical vocabularies.
- As part of business process management, the process-oriented information systems in health-care (ProHealth) view focuses on using business process management technology to provide effective solutions for the management of health-care processes. This community aims at adapting successful process management solutions to health-care processes and needs, with a particular interest in organization, optimization, cooperation, risk analysis, flexibility, re-utilization, and integration of health-care tasks and teams.

For a fourth time, this workshop brought together researchers from the previously mentioned two communities who have been addressing these challenges from different perspectives. The knowledge representation (KR) for health-care community, which is part of the larger medical informatics community, aims at developing knowledge representation and reasoning systems to support knowledge management and clinical decision-making. In the past this community has worked to build efficient representations, technologies, and tools for integrating all the important computer elements required to provide modern health care. Some of these are: EMRs and health-care information systems, clinical practice guidelines, and standardized medical vocabularies. In turn, the community about process-oriented information systems in health-care, which is part of the larger business process management (BPM) community, aims to adopt BPM technologies to implement solutions for health-care process management. KR and BPM technologies are mutually complementary to provide a holistic approach to the health-care sector, which is currently demanding intelligent computer solutions to improve their clinical procedures, to increase clinical practice safety, and to homogenize clinical interventions.

In 2012, 2013, and 2015 joint workshops were organized bringing together health-care knowledge representation as dealt with in previous KR4HC workshops, and health-care process support as addressed in previous ProHealth workshops, with a considerable success. Participants in the joint workshops could explore the potential and the limitations of the two approaches for supporting health-care knowledge and process management and clinical decision-making. The workshops also provided a forum wherein challenges, paradigms, and tools for optimized knowledge-based clinical process support could be debated. All the organizers and participants of the workshops agreed on the profit of the event, which encouraged us to organize a fourth edition of the joint workshop in 2016.

With the same general objectives of these previous workshop, the fourth joint workshop was made to increase interactions between researchers and practitioners from these complementary fields. In this new forum we wanted to offer stakeholders the opportunity not only to improve the understanding of domain-specific requirements, methods, theories, tools, and techniques, but also to explore how the approaches from the two communities could be better integrated.

The KR4HC/ProHealth 2016 received 12 papers from Europe (Belgium, France, Germany, Greece, Israel, Luxemburg, The Netherlands, Spain, and UK), Asia (China and Hong Kong), and America (USA). Papers had to clearly establish their research contribution as well as their benefits to health care. Six papers were selected to be presented at the workshop as long presentations, according to their relevance, quality, and originality. Three more papers were selected for short presentations, after the expert review recommendations. Only the six full papers appear in this volume, together with a paper by the keynote speaker, Dr. Jesualdo Tomás Fernández-Breis.

In his challenging keynote presentation "Can Existing Biomedical Ontologies Be More Useful for EHR and DSS?," Dr. Fernández-Breis from the Faculty of Computer Science at the University of Murcia (Spain), exposed the increasing benefits of using biomedical ontologies in health care. He foresaw a next-generation EHR and decision support systems in which ontologies will be fundamental for enabling interoperability. He also dug into the main technological issues that need to be solved in order to make biomedical ontologies useful for EHR and DSS, and presented relevant and promising contributions to this end.

We would like to conclude by expressing our gratitude to the invited speaker for his participation, and the members of the Program Committee for their support selecting the best papers. All of them helped us to compile a high-quality program for the KR4HC/ProHealth 2016 workshop.

We hope you will find our selection of the papers of the joint KR4HC/ProHealth 2016 workshop included in this volume interesting and stimulating.

December 2016

David Riaño
Richard Lenz
Manfred Reichert

Organization

KR4HC/ProHealth 2016 was organized by David Riaño, Universitat Rovira i Virgili, Spain, Richard Lenz, University of Erlangen-Nuremberg, Germany, and Manfred Reichert, University of Ulm, Germany.

Program Committee

Syed Sibte Raza Abidi	Dalhousie University, Canada
Luca Anselma	Università di Torino, Italy
Joseph Barjis	Delft University of Technology, The Netherlands
Arturo González Ferrer	University Carlos III of Madrid, Spain
David Isern	Universitat Rovira i Virgili, Spain
Stefan Jablonski	University of Bayreuth, Germany
Vassilis Koutkias	Institut National de la Santé et de la Recherche Médicale, France
Peter Lucas	Radboud University Nijmegen, The Netherlands
Wendy MacCaull	St. Francis Xavier University, Canada
Mar Marcos	Universitat Jaume I, Spain
Stephanie Medlock	Academic Medical Center, University of Amsterdam, The Netherlands
Silvia Miksch	Vienna University of Technology, Austria
Stefania Montani	University of Piemonte Orientale, Italy
Øystein Nytrø	Norwegian University of Science and Technology, Norway
Leon Osterweil	University of Massachusetts Amherst, USA
Mor Peleg	University of Haifa, Israel
Danielle Sent	AMC/UvA, The Netherlands
Brigitte Seroussi	Hôpitaux de Paris, France
Yuval Shahar	Ben Gurion University, Israel
Ton Spil	University of Twente, The Netherlands
Maria Taboada	University of Santiago de Compostela, Spain
Annette Ten Teije	VU University Amsterdam, The Netherlands
Paolo Terenziani	Università del Piemonte Orientale Amedeo Avogadro, Italy
Lucinéia Heloisa Thom	Federal University of Rio Grande do Sul, Brazil
Frank van Harmelen	Vrije Universiteit Amsterdam, The Netherlands
Dongwen Wang	University of Rocherster, USA
Barbara Weber	University of Innsbruck, Austria
Szymon Wilk	Poznan University of Technology, Poland

Contents

Ontologies in Health Care

Can Existing Biomedical Ontologies Be More Useful for EHR and CDS?

Jesualdo Tomás Fernández-Breis[✉], Manuel Quesada-Martínez,
and Astrid Duque-Ramos

Facultad de Informática, Instituto Murciano de Investigación Biosanitaria,
IMIB-Arrixaca-UMU, Universidad de Murcia, Campus de Espinardo,
30100 Murcia, Spain
{jfernand,manuel.quesada,astrid.duque}@um.es

Abstract. The interoperability of Electronic Health Records (EHR) and Clinical Decision Support (CDS) systems is a major challenge in the medical informatics field. International initiatives propose the use of ontologies for bridging both types of systems. The next-generation of EHR and CDS systems are supposed to use ontologies, or at least ontologies should be fundamental for enabling their interoperability. This situation makes necessary to analyze if current ontologies are ready for playing such intended role. In this paper we describe and discuss some important issues that need to be solved in order to have optimal ontologies for such a purpose, such as the need for increasing reuse in ontologies, as well as getting axiomatically richer ontologies. We also describe how our recent research results in the areas of ontology enrichment and ontology evaluation may contribute to such a goal.

Keywords: Electronic Health Records · Clinical decision-support systems · Semantic interoperability · Ontology quality · Ontology enrichment

1 Introduction

Humans have been interested in recording information about patient care for many years and even centuries (see for instance [6,13]). The development of the information and communication technologies has permitted to store and exchange the medical information in electronic formats, which has generated new opportunities for improving clinical research and the quality of health care.

Two relevant types of medical information systems are Electronic Health Records (EHR) and Clinical Decision Support (CDS). EHR systems provide the means for storing the medical information generated by the interactions of patients with the health system. In the most generic way, the EHR of a patient should provide access to all the medical information of the patient, that is, from all the healthcare institutions in which the patient has received care. Unfortunately, this is not possible due to the lack of interoperability between

© Springer International Publishing AG 2017
D. Riaño et al. (Eds.): KR4HC/ProHealth 2016, LNAI 10096, pp. 3–20, 2017.
DOI: 10.1007/978-3-319-55014-5_1

different EHR systems. CDS systems try to help physicians in the diagnosis and treatment of patients, basically by combining the medical knowledge with the patient data. Consequently, CDS systems should have access to the content of the EHR and, similarly, to have access to the recommendations of CDS systems from the EHR system would be helpful for physicians.

As it will be described in Sect. 2, there has been a significant evolution of EHR and CDS systems, but such evolution has not achieved an effective communication between those systems. The interoperability of EHR and CDS systems is indeed an existing challenge for the medical informatics community and it has been the subject of reports of international efforts and initiatives such as Semantic HealthNet (SHN)[1].

In the last years, the Semantic Web technologies have gained popularity in the pursuit of the semantic interoperability of health information systems, especially since the Semantic Health project [17] recommended the use of ontologies for supporting semantic interoperability in healthcare. The Semantic Web [4] is a natural space for data integration based on shared meaning [12] in which the shared models of meaning are provided by ontologies. SHN also proposes that ontological formalization should be fundamental for enabling a meaningful exchange and cooperation between EHR and CDS systems. The meaningful exchange between EHR and CDS systems also imposes a series of requirements on biomedical ontologies related to knowledge representation, data retrieval and classification.

In this paper, we examine how current biomedical ontologies meet such requirements, which will determine to what extent current biomedical ontologies are useful for bridging between EHR and CDS systems. Besides, we describe two frameworks developed by our research group that contribute to increase the usefulness of biomedical ontologies. We believe that these frameworks can be part of the solution but additional actions are also required. We believe that this work permits to gain knowledge on the types of actions that will make possible the effective ontology-based interoperability of EHR and CDS systems.

2   Background

In this section we provide an overview of the evolution of EHR and CDS systems, including how the interaction between ontologies and such systems has been addressed in the last years.

2.1   EHR Systems

The first experiences of electronic medical records happened in the sixties, when the Akron Children's hospital and IBM collaborated to develop a computer-based patient information system [32] with the aim of centralising medical information, sharing information and reducing paperwork. Since then, EHR systems

---

[1] http://www.semantichealthnet.eu.

have evolved in many different ways, and today we can see how physicians can input or have access to the patient records by using tablets or smartphones [21]. This is clearly an advance in the way of interacting with the EHR content, but its real impact depends on what can be effectively done from such modern interfaces. Computer-based records share with paper-based ones the heterogeneity in structure and content, which makes difficult for computers to understand and to process the content of the EHR, and so limiting the practical usefulness of EHR systems.

The information architecture of EHR systems is fundamental for the useful exploitation of EHR data, and there has also been an evolution in the architecture of EHR systems in the last decades. EHR systems have been studied as a subsystem of knowledge management [20]. From such perspective, four generations of systems can be distinguished. The first generation did not include any possibility for representing knowledge. The systems from the second generation started to provide some capabilities for knowledge representation. The integration with clinical decision and the availability of purpose-specific knowledge bases started to happen in the third generation. Finally, the fourth generation uses formal knowledge representation languages.

From an information architecture point of view, the early EHR systems followed the single-level methodological approach. In a single-level approach, the medical experts discuss with the software engineers the requirements and needs of the EHR systems, and all the medical knowledge is implemented in the EHR system. In this context, implemented has to be understood as hard-coded, since in most cases the medical knowledge was fixed in the system, and updating the knowledge usually requires major implementation changes in the EHR system. This is obviously a suboptimal decision given the current progress of science and medicine, which requires EHR systems capable to work in a context of dynamic, evolving knowledge.

In the nineties, the Good European Health Record (GEHR) project [14], funded by European Health Telematics research, had as main objective to achieve a generic representation of EHR data that would enable data exchange between EHR systems. Its most popular result was the dual-level methodology for the development of EHR systems. This methodology innovates in the relation between the medical knowledge and the EHR system, because now the EHR system uses the medical knowledge, but this is not hard-coded into the system. This means that the knowledge can be updated without requiring major implementation changes. This architecture has inspired the development of specifications and standards such as openEHR[2], ISO 13606[3] or HL7 CDA[4]. This is the architecture of the next generation of EHR systems, which is based on standards.

The dual-level methodology uses two modelling levels: information and knowledge. The information level provides the modeling primitives for representing, storing and exchanging EHR data. The knowledge level provides the

---

[2] http://www.openehr.org.
[3] http://www.iso.org/iso/catalogue_detail.htm?csnumber=40784.
[4] http://www.hl7.org/implement/standards/product_brief.cfm?product_id=7.

clinical models, which define data structures that will be used for capturing the EHR data in a particular scenario. By clinical model we refer to artifacts such as archetypes [3], CEMs[5], FHIR resources[6] or CIMI models[7], since they are the technological solution for the knowledge level proposed by the different specifications. The clinical models facilitate the meaningful exchange of EHR data between systems, because the meaning of the data captured is provided by means of links to semantic resources. For simplicity, we focus next on archetypes.

Archetypes contain a terminology (formerly ontology) section, which is used to provide the specific meaning to the information. In this section we may define that the valid values for the field "blood phenotype" is a query over SNOMED CT[8]. Such association is described using an archetype constraint. This constraint is a query that would show the user all the SNOMED CT concepts that are the result of the query. However, once the corresponding code is chosen, it is stored and used in the EHR system as a code, since the technologies used in archetypes-based systems are not able to natively exploit the semantics of resources such as SNOMED CT. This situation is not exclusive for archetypes, but it also happens with other types of clinical models. The answer to such semantic limitation provided by a part of the research community has been to propose the use of semantic formalisms, such as the Web Ontology Language (OWL) as the common formalism for expressing the reference model, the clinical information models and the semantic resources used by the former ones [18,19,34].

2.2 CDS Systems

The history of computerized clinical decision support (CDS) systems also starts in the late fifties/early sixties. The Warner system [37] was one of the earliest decision support systems, developed for the diagnosis of congenital heart disease using data from more than 1000 patients. The increasing complexity of medical knowledge and the amount and types of information sources needed to support clinical decisions has driven the evolution of CDS systems, with the traditional objective of having the EHR as the reference source of information. In [39], the evolution of CDS systems is described using four phases of evolution: (1) stand-alone systems, which are independent of the EHR system; (2) integrated systems, which are integrated into clinical information systems, but not necessarily with the EHR; (3) standards-based systems, which include the use of standards to represent, encode, store and share knowledge; and (4) service models, in which CDS and EHR are connected through interfaces. The last two phases are the most relevant ones for our purpose because they describe a context in which CDS systems are based on standards and provide ways for communicating and exchanging information. If we focus on computerized clinical guidelines, a series of languages and frameworks such as Arden [1], GLIF [23] or PROForma [11]

---

[5] http://informatics.mayo.edu/sharp/index.php/CEMS.

[6] https://www.hl7.org/fhir/.

[7] http://www.opencimi.org/.

[8] http://www.ihtsdo.org/snomed-ct.

have been proposed in the last decades. They provide ways for expressing clinical knowledge, expressing and executing clinical guidelines, but they cannot easily be connected with the EHR. One of the main reasons was identified in [15]: "The inclusion of a guideline-based system into an existing electronic medical record system is hard because they are designed as a closed monolithic system with a lack of interoperability methods." Basically, this means that despite EHR and CDS systems use standards to represent the medical knowledge required, such standards are not really interoperable, which limits the joint operation of EHR and CDS systems.

Recently, the Guideline Definition Language (GDL) [7] was proposed by the openEHR Foundation to palliate this situation. GDL is a formal language for expressing decision support logic, and closely related to the openEHR Reference Model (RM) and Archetype Model (AM). GDL proposes to specify the decision support logic using the entities provided by the openEHR RM and AM. Consequently, the queries described in the guideline would be compatible with the structure of the EHR and, therefore, CDS systems could effectively reuse the EHR data.

In Sect. 2.1 we have mentioned that EHR standards based on archetypes are limited in the processing of the semantics associated with the data and the clinical information models. The logic included in the guidelines may need to perform inferences, which requires to be able to exploit the semantics of all the information involved. Consequently, to date, approaches such as GDL keep having the drawback of their limited exploitation of the semantics of the resources used for providing the meaning to the data.

Ontologies have been used in CDS systems in the last years. In the nineties, ontologies were already used to support protocol-based decisions [36], and we can find a number of papers with related use since then [5,10,22,40]. The specification of guidelines was also approached using ontologies, see for instance [31]. More recently, ontologies have been proposed to drive the execution of the guideline [16], and to mediate between the guideline and the medical knowledge [38]. However, none of them solve the integration of EHR and CDS systems. Interestingly, according to the results of the review presented in [24], the integration of clinical guidelines with the EHR has not been one of the most active areas in the period 2001–2013.

3   Ontologies in the Interface EHR-CDS

The evolution of EHR and CDS systems reveals that ontologies are gaining momentum. This is supported by the fact that clinical models may use ontologies for providing the semantics to the data, the existing experiences in the use of ontologies and semantic web technologies for representing clinical models and EHR data, and that ontologies have been used for modelling and driving the execution of computerized clinical guidelines. However, the integration of EHR and CDS systems remains unsolved.

We could ask ourselves whether ontologies could be an effective bridge for EHR and CDS systems. This question is not novel, since the central role of ontologies for connecting EHR and CDS systems has been proposed ealier. [29] describes the relations between the patient data model (information model), the concept model (ontology), and the guideline model (inference model). This vision proposes that clear interfaces between these models are required in order to get interoperability between EHR and CDS systems. Moreover, an interface between the three models is also needed. Whereas ontologies provide the static domain knowledge, guidelines provide the dynamic one, which means that both should use the same building blocks, and share the same concepts, that is, use a common knowledge model.

[29] makes a statement that reinforces the role of ontologies in the interface EHR-CDS: "The concept model should be capable of classifying the information of the medical record under the abstractions used in the guideline". A practical interpretation of this statement is that if the medical record contains a blood pressure measurement of an individual of 190/110 and the guideline manages the concept "elevated blood pressure", then the concept model (ontology) should be capable of classifying that individual as a "person with elevated blood pressure". Consequently, the ontology would be the bridge between the EHR data and the CDS knowledge.

Semantic HealthNet (SHN)[9] has been an EU FP7 Network of Excellence which has run in the period 2011–2015. SHN identified four major axes of activity for the "consistent representation, access and interpretation" of health data: (1) data and record structure and content; (2) workflow; (3) terminology systems; and (4) privacy. An analysis of the content of each axe shows a close relation between the first three ones and the models proposed in [29]. The SHN deliverables[10] 4.4 and 4.5 also contain some statements reinforcing the role of ontologies in the interface EHR-CDS:

- The information model must hold the patient information necessary to determine whether certain clinical guidelines criteria are satisfied.
- Clinical models and clinical guidelines must share the same ontology for representing their concepts.
- Guideline creators should map their non-standardized vocabularies to standardized ontologies.
- The elements of clinical models should be mapped to standardized ontologies and used in the guidelines.

The potential role of ontologies as a bridge between EHR and CDS systems has been described in previous sections. This helps us to understand the usefulness of an ontology in this context, which we approach as to what extent a given ontology may play such role. Given that bridging between EHR and CDS can be too generic, the following specific requirements for usefulness can be identified:

---

[9] http://www.semantichealthnet.eu.
[10] http://www.semantichealthnet.eu/index.cfm/deliverables.

1. Representation, sharing and reuse of knowledge for information and inference models.
2. Classification of EHR data according to guideline rules.
3. EHR data retrieval according to guideline rules.
4. Quality-assured ontology.

The first three requirements can be drawn from the content of the previous sections, but the fourth one comes from the need of using quality-proof artifacts in legacy health information systems. In the remaining of this section, an analysis of the usefulness of current biomedical ontologies is performed. The results of such analysis will be the input for revising and proposing methods for increasing the usefulness of ontologies.

Performing a systematic analysis of ontologies requires to define, measure and evaluate a series of indicators that would capture our intended meaning of usefulness. The ontology engineering community has not been able to reach a consensus on a series of metrics that should be used for the analysis of a given ontology. The number of classes, properties, axioms, labels, or the visits to the ontology are some indicators that have been traditionally measured and evaluated in ontologies, although they do not generate enough information for our purpose. Initiatives such as the OBO Foundry [33] have proposed a series of good design principles for biomedical ontologies. Among such criteria we can identify three that can be useful for our objective:

- Delineated content: The OBO Foundry promotes the development of an orthogonal collection of biomedical ontologies. This means that biomedical ontologies should reuse the content from other existing ontologies to avoid overlaps.
- Relations: There should be a consistent formulation of relational assertions, which is related to the number and types of relations used in biomedical ontologies. This aspect will be approached in a more general way, since the types of axioms, not only relations, will be analyzed.
- Naming conventions: The labels associated with the concepts in the ontology should be meaningful for humans. Besides, there should be lexical relations between the labels of taxonomically related concepts. Since a taxonomic child concept is a specialization of its parent, then the label of the child concept could be an extension of the label of the parent.

Next, a summary of the results of analyzing more than 200 OWL ontologies retrieved from BioPortal is presented, whereas the complete results can be found in related papers [26, 27].

Reuse. The analysis of how ontology content is being reused by other ontologies has a direct implication on the requirement 1, that is, on the representation, sharing and reuse of knowledge. Besides, reuse can be approached from two different perspectives, namely, effective and potential reuse.

Effective reuse is measured by taking into account how many ontologies are imported and reused. Our results show that only 23% of the ontologies analyzed reuse content from other ontologies, 90% of which reuse only one ontology. Both results are a sign of low effective reuse in biomedical ontologies. However, some positive findings were also obtained in this analysis. The most frequently reused ontologies are the Basic Formal Ontology (BFO)[11], the OBO Relations Ontology[12] and the Information Artifact Ontology (IAO)[13]. Those ontologies can be considered top-level or very general knowledge frameworks, so their frequent reuse means that many ontologies are using a common background knowledge, which positively contributes to requirement 1.

Potential reuse identifies content from other ontologies that could be reused in a given ontology by performing lexical matches between the content of the labels of the classes. Three types of matches are taken into account:

- Internal exact match (IEM): The lexical regularity is the full label of another class of the same ontology. For example, there is an internal exact match between the class "amine binding" and "binding" if both classes are in the same ontology. In this case, reuse would mean that the class "binding" could be used for defining the axioms associated with the class "amine binding".
- External exact match (EEM): The lexical regularity is the full label of a class of a different ontology. For example, there is an external exact match between the class "peptide antigen binding" in the Gene Ontology [2] and "antigen" in SNOMED CT. In this case, the class "antigen" could be used for defining the axioms associated with the class "peptide antigen binding".
- External regularity match (ERM): The lexical regularity is also a regularity in a different ontology. For example, there is an external regularity match between the class "peptide antigen binding" in the Gene Ontology and "antigen role" in OBI, since "antigen" is a shared regularity. In this case, the semantics associated with "antigen" could be used for defining the axioms associated with the two classes of this ERM.

The first step in the analysis of potential reuse was to calculate the regularities existing in the labels of the classes of our corpus. For this study, only those regularities with frequency greater than 1% were used, in this case, 8175 regularities. Then, we calculated the IEM, EEM and ERM for all the classes in the corpus. The results were that 15.60% of the regularities had IEMs, 36.44% of the regularities had EEMs, and 23.49% of the regularities had ERMs. These results clearly show that there is a huge potential reuse in biomedical ontologies, which is yet to be exploited.

Axioms. The analysis of the axiomatic richness of an ontology is closely related to requirements 2–3, that is, the classification and retrieval of data. It is also related to the fourth one, since the axiomatization of the ontology has traditionally been linked to the quality of ontologies. Besides, it is related to the machine understandability of the content of the ontology.

---

[11] http://www.obofoundry.org/ontology/bfo.html.

[12] http://www.obofoundry.org/ontology/ro.html.

[13] http://www.obofoundry.org/ontology/iao.html.

This study has focused on the analysis of the types of axioms used in the corpus of ontologies analyzed. The results reveal that the most frequently used type of axiom is Annotation Assertion (57.63%), followed by subClassOf (26.84%). Hence, two types of axioms (out of 35 types of axioms in OWL2) cover more than 84% of the axioms defined in this corpus.

Annotation axioms provide content that is basically in natural language such as labels, comments or descriptions, so that content cannot be easily used by the machine. The taxonomic relation provides the hierarchical structure of the ontologies, so most ontologies in this corpus can be described as plain taxonomies rich in natural language content. Consequently, its axiomatic richness is lower than expected to fulfil our usefulness requirements.

Systematic Naming. The analysis of the application of a systematic naming convention is directly related to the understandability of the content of the ontology for humans, but we also see it related to the axiomatization of the ontology due to the potential reuse in biomedical ontologies. There are tools such as Ontocheck [30] that permit to test the application of naming conventions in ontologies. Basically, the application of naming conventions implies that there is an agreement on how to name and label the classes. In practical terms, the application of the naming convention implies that taxonomically related classes should have similar linguistic labels, and the labels of the child concepts should be extensions of the labels of the parent ones. Consequently, the systematic naming of classes must have an impact on the regularity of the content of the labels and on the number of words repeated in different labels. Our study focused on the analysis of the regularities as a sign of the application of a systematic naming convention in our corpus. We found that the percentage of repeated words in the labels was 67.7%, all the ontologies having values over 50% and the maximum reaching 94.7%. The existence of regularities with length over 10 words is also a clear sign of application of naming conventions.

4   Increasing the Usefulness of Ontologies

Two main limitations of existing biomedical ontologies can be identified from our usefulness perspective: effective reuse and axiomatization. However, it is worth to study whether the results obtained in terms of potential reuse and systematic naming conventions can be used for overcoming such limitations. For this purpose, we performed a clustering of the ontologies in the corpus described in previous sections. We performed an agglomerative hierarchical clustering (k-means) by taking into account three variables: percentage of classes with regularities, percentage of classes with IEM or EEM matches, and percentage of repeated words. The inspection of the dendrogram suggested the existence of three differentiated groups of ontologies.

Figure 1 shows the spatial distribution of the ontologies and the three clusters. Cluster 1 contains 43% of the ontologies, Cluster 2 33% and Cluster 3 24%. Cluster 1 includes ontologies with many regularities, many repeated words and those ontologies with the highest percentage of matches. Cluster 2 includes those ontologies with many repeated words and high degree of regularity. Cluster 3 includes the ontologies with the lowest values for the three variables. We think that the axiomatic richness and reuse in the ontologies of Clusters 1 and 2 could be addressed by analyzing and exploiting the regularities and matches existing in such ontologies. This conclusion is reinforced by the distance between the clusters depicted in the figure. In the next subsections we describe two frameworks that can contribute to increase the usefulness of biomedical ontologies. First, we need to facilitate the reuse of ontologies. This requires facilitating the task of identifying which ontology provides the best knowledge for the new ontology. This support is needed because the current set of existing biomedical ontologies is not orthogonal. Second, we need to support ontology developers in creating axiomatically-rich ontologies and in evaluating and assuring the quality of their ontologies. These frameworks deal with (1) ontology enrichment and (2) ontology evaluation. The first one has the objective of identifying and analyzing the regularities in the content and structure of the labels in biomedical ontologies, and to find content from other ontologies that could be used for adding or improving existing axioms in ontologies. The second one has the objective of identifying strengths and flaws in ontologies from an engineering perspective.

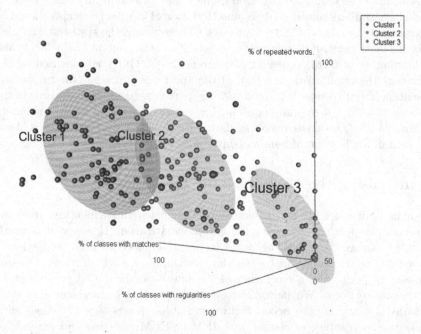

Fig. 1. 3D scatterplot of the clusters obtained with more than 200 BioPortal ontologies

4.1   Ontology Enrichment

This process takes advantage of the fact that biomedical ontologies have hidden semantics [35], that is, some content of the ontologies is only expressed in natural language, but not as logical axioms. Consequently, such content is only available for humans, not for machines. This ontology enrichment method, called OntoEnrich, is inspired by the "lexically suggest, logically define" principle [28], which means that what is expressed in natural language for humans should be expressed in the form of axioms for the machines.

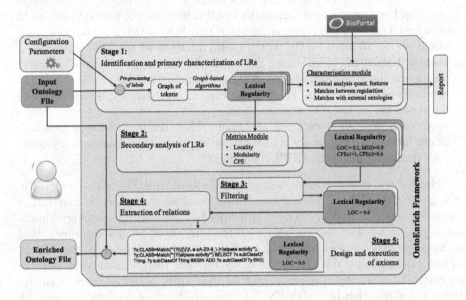

Fig. 2. Diagram of the different stages of the ontology enrichment framework

Figure 2 shows the stages included in our ontology enrichment approach:

- Stage 1: Identification and basic characterization of lexical regularities. The content of the labels of the classes of biomedical ontologies is processed using Natural Language Processing techniques to identify the lexical regularities, which are ordered, consecutive words that appear in different labels. This stage selects the regularities whose frequency is over a user-defined threshold. The primary characterization also finds the IEM, EEM, and ERM with the ontologies existing in BioPortal.
- Stage 2: Advanced characterization of lexical regularities. A series of metrics are calculated for each regularity: locality, modularity and cross-products extensions (CPE). Locality accounts for how close the classes that exhibit a given regularity are in the ontology. The enrichment of the classes associated with regularities with high locality would affect a particular region of the ontology. Modularity analyses the distribution of the regularity in selected modules

of the ontology, which permits to identify which modules are associated with the regularity. In this context, a module refers to a subontology, and it is identified by its root class. The CPE analyses to what extent the content of the regularity has matches with classes from the same or different ontologies. For example, if the content of the regularity can be fully decomposed in matching classes, then the axioms associated with the regularity could be defined by reusing existing classes.

- Stage 3: Filtering lexical regularities. The analysis of the metrics associated with the lexical regularities may help the ontology developer to filter out the regularities less promising for the enrichment of the ontology. Besides filters based on frequency, locality, modality or CPE metrics, the method permits to filter based on the super/subrelations that may hold between regularities. This would permit to focus on the most general or the most specific regularities.
- Stage 4: Extraction of relations. The method is able to automatically suggest taxonomic links between classes sharing a regularity. This requires that the regularity matches the full label of one class in the ontology, which would be the superclass in those taxonomic links.
- Stage 5: Design and execution of axioms. The user may define a template axiom for a given regularity, which can be applied to the classes that exhibit such regularity using the OPPL2 language[14].

This method has been implemented and made available online in our OntoEnrich platform[15]. There, the results of a series of analyses can be found. The "lexically suggest, logically define" principle has inspired our ontology enrichment process but can also be used with the purpose of quality assurance, that is, to check that the logical axioms have the meaning expressed in the content in natural language. We have actually applied our method with such purpose on SNOMED CT, and this has permitted to identify potential cases of suboptimal axiomatization in SNOMED CT [25], which would lead to queries with incomplete results if issued against EHR datasets.

4.2 Ontology Quality Evaluation: The OQuaRE Framework

Assuring the quality of ontologies requires to perform a series of different types of analyses over them, which would measure different properties of the ontologies. Many ontology evaluation methods have traditionally been applied with the objective of ranking ontologies for a given purpose, although we approach it from the perspective of identifying strengths and flaws in biomedical ontologies. Such findings should help the ontology developers to improve their ontologies, and ontology users to select the ontologies that provides the best match to their requirements. It should be noted that quality evaluation tasks are usually understood as objective evaluations to test to what extent a determined product meets some requirements.

---

[14] http://oppl2.sourceforge.net.
[15] http://sele.inf.um.es/ontoenrich.

In the last years we have designed and developed an objective, reproducible, quantitative framework for evaluating the quality of ontologies, which is called OQuaRE [8]. OQuaRE is adapted from SQuaRE[16], an international standard for software product quality evaluation. The complete description of the OQuaRE framework can be found in its website[17], although its main features are described next. OQuaRE structures the evaluation of the quality of an ontology using four out of the five divisions proposed by SQuaRE: quality evaluation, quality requirements, quality model (characteristics and subcharacteristics) and quality measurements. OQuaRE uses the eight quality characteristics proposed by SQuaRE for measuring software quality: functional adequacy, reliability, operability, maintainability, compatibility, transferability, performance efficiency and quality in use. Besides, OQuaRE adds the structural characteristic, because of the relevance of structural aspects in the quality of ontologies. Each quality characteristic has a set of associated quality subcharacteristics, which are measured through quality metrics. The values of the quality metrics are automatically calculated.

The current version of OQuaRE includes 9 characteristics, 49 subcharacteristics and 16 metrics. The values of the metrics are scaled to the range $[1, 5]$, which has been traditionally used in quality evaluation frameworks. The weighted mean of the metrics scores associated with each subcharacteristic permits to assign a $[1, 5]$ score to each quality subcharacteristic. The quality scores of each quality characteristic are obtained by the weighted average of the scores of its subcharacteristics. Although it is possible to calculate a quality score for the whole ontology, we think that such score is not relevant for our purpose of showing strengths and flaws, but for the application of the framework with the purpose of ranking ontologies. Consequently, the quality scores could guide the process of deciding which ontology to reuse, since the scores should permit the users to make informed decisions by matching their requirements to the ontologies' scores.

It would be expected that an axiomatically richer ontology would have better quality scores for certain properties. This was shown by the application of OQuaRE to two different versions of the Cell Type Ontology [8]. One version, called oCTO, was the original Cell Type Ontology. The second version, called nCTO, was the result of a redesign of the ontology, including more axioms. Figure 3 shows the scores of the quality characteristics for both ontologies. The results show that nCTO obtains higher scores for most characteristics, what has an implication on the practical usefulness of both ontologies. Besides, a method such as OQuaRE should contribute to analyze whether changes in the ontologies have the expected impact on the quality characteristics. Recently, we have developed an extension of the OQuaRE framework which is capable of analyzing the evolution of an ontology [9]. Figure 4 shows the evolution of the values of selected metrics (TMOnto, NOMOnto, RFCOnto, LCOMOnto, RROnto) for a

---

[16] http://www.iso.org/iso/iso_catalogue/catalogue_tc/catalogue_detail.htm? csnumber=35683.

[17] http://sele.inf.um.es/oquare.

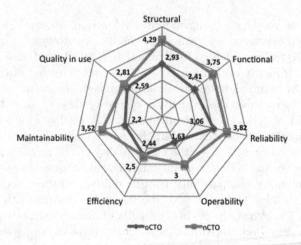

Fig. 3. Radar graph showing the quality scores of seven OQuaRE quality characteristics for both versions of the Cell Type Ontology

biomedical ontology. In the figure, each line represents the evolution of the quality scores (scale 1–5) of each metric across the eighteen versions of EDAM. We can observe that the quality scores of some metrics vary significantly between the initial versions and the final ones. Besides, it can be seen that version 4 is key because this version triggers most of the major changes in the quality scores. The inspection of that version reveals that there was a change in the modeling style for some properties in the ontology, and such design decision had an impact on the metrics. Frameworks such as OQuaRE permits ontology developers to analyze the changes made in their ontologies from a quality evaluation perspective. This helps them to check whether the effects are in line with the requirements for their ontologies, which contributes to achieve higher quality, more useful biomedical ontologies.

5   Discussion and Conclusions

In this paper we have described the evolution of EHR and CDS systems, illustrating why their meaningful communication has not been reached yet. According to the international recommendations, ontologies should play an important role for enabling such meaningful communication, which led us to briefly analyzed how ontologies have been used in EHR and CDS systems, and identifying some requirements ontologies should meet in order to be useful for bridging between EHR and CDS systems. Some results analyzing how existing ontologies meet those requirements were presented, identifying a series of improvements in biomedical ontologies for optimizing their efficacy for playing the intended bridging role: (1) the reuse of content from standardized ontologies, which should help to

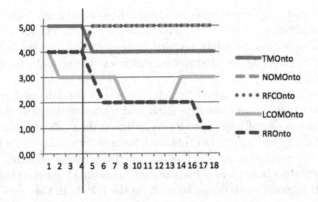

Fig. 4. Evolution of the values of the metrics across the different versions of an ontology

build the knowledge required to capture and describe EHR data and the clinical guidelines, (2) increasing the axiomatization of ontologies to improve data retrieval and classification; and (3) assuring the quality of ontologies as products.

We have described two frameworks that have demonstrated in the last years that they can help to increase the usefulness of biomedical ontologies. The ontology enrichment framework, implemented in the OntoEnrich platform, pursues to convert the hidden semantics existing in the labels of biomedical ontologies into explicit knowledge, that is, logical axioms. This framework contributes to the reuse of content by identifying matches between classes from different ontologies since it includes algorithms for token-based lexical alignment. Besides, it contributes to the axiomatization of ontologies because its methods permit to design new logical axioms that can be added to a set of classes in the ontology. Finally, this framework can also contribute to quality assurance, since it permits to analyze how principles such as "lexically suggest, logically define" are applied. The ontology evaluation framework, implemented in the OQuaRE platform, contributes to the quality assurance of the ontology by providing quantitative information to ontology developers about the strengths and flaws of the ontologies during their whole development, since it permits to analyze the effects of changes in different versions of an ontology. Moreover, reuse can also be supported by OQuaRE, since its quantitative information can be applied by users for making informed decisions about which content to reuse.

Nevertheless, these are only two of the processes needed to increase the usefulness of biomedical ontologies. For example, one of the requirements for biomedical ontologies is reusing standardized ontologies, including top-level ontologies such as BFO[18] or BioTop[19]. Despite our results show that BFO is the most reused ontology, the size and modeling style of top-level ontologies is not handled by ontology tools in an optimal way, what makes difficult to explore and find the right classes. We also believe that EHR standards and CDS frameworks

---

[18] http://www.obofoundry.org/ontology/bfo.html.
[19] http://purl.bioontology.org/ontology/BT.

should be rethought to be grounded on standardized ontologies. This would help to overcome limitations such as the ones described in current archetype-based technology. That would certainly require agreements on the semantic modeling primitives for both types of systems, which would certainly facilitate their interoperability.

In summary, biomedical ontologies should play a fundamental role for the meaningful exchange of data between EHR and CDS systems, but they need to be improved in a series of ways in order to optimize their efficacy and efficiency. The notion of usefulness applied in this work focuses on making more knowledge available for the machines and in facilitating the reuse of content, but other complementary aspects must also be taken into account. We hope that the work described in this paper contributes to gear up the efforts in this area.

Acknowledgements. This work has been partially funded by to the Spanish Ministry of Economy and Competitiveness, the FEDER Programme and by the Fundación Séneca through grants TIN2014-53749-C2-2-R and 19371/PI/14.

References

1. Health Level 7.: Arden Syntax for Medical Logic Systems Standard Version 2.6. Ann Arbor, MI: Health Level 7 (2007)
2. Ashburner, M., Ball, C.A., Blake, J.A., Botstein, D., Butler, H., Cherry, J.M., Davis, A.P., Dolinski, K., Dwight, S.S., Eppig, J.T., et al.: Gene ontology: tool for the unification of biology. Nature Genet. **25**(1), 25–29 (2000)
3. Beale, T.: Archetypes: constraint-based domain models for future-proof information systems. In: OOPSLA 2002 Workshop on Behavioural Semantics, vol. 105 (2002)
4. Berners-Lee, T., Hendler, J., Lassila, O., et al.: The semantic web. Sci. Am. **284**(5), 28–37 (2001)
5. Bouamrane, M.-M., Rector, A., Hurrell, M.: Using owl ontologies for adaptive patient information modelling and preoperative clinical decision support. Knowl. Inform. Syst. **29**(2), 405–418 (2011)
6. Breasted, J.H.: The Edwin Smith Surgical Papyrus: published in facsimile and hieroglyphic transliteration with translation and commentary in two volumes, vol. 3. Chic. UP (1930)
7. Chen, R., Corbal, I.: Guideline definition language (gdl). Release 0.9, pp. 1–23 (2013)
8. Duque-Ramos, A., Fernández-Breis, J.T., Stevens, R., Aussenac-Gilles, R.N., et al.: Oquare: a square-based approach for evaluating the quality of ontologies. J. Res. Pract. Inform. Technol. **43**(2), 159 (2011)
9. Duque-Ramos, A., Quesada-Martínez, M., Iniesta-Moreno, M., Fernández-Breis, J.T., Stevens, R.: Supporting the analysis of ontology evolution processes through the combination of static and dynamic scaling functions in oquare. J. Biomed. Semant. **7**(1), 63 (2016)
10. Farion, K., Michalowski, W., Wilk, S., O'Sullivan, D.M., Rubin, S., Weiss, D.: Clinical decision support system for point of care use: ontology driven design and software implementation. Meth. Inform. Med. **48**(4), 381–390 (2009)

11. Fox, J., Johns, N., Rahmanzadeh, A.: Disseminating medical knowledge: the proforma approach. Artif. Intell. Med. **14**(1), 157–182 (1998)
12. Goble, C., Stevens, R.: Stevens.: state of the nation in data integration for bioinformatics. J. Biomed. Inform. **41**(5), 687–693 (2008)
13. Hawkins, M., Ralley, R., Young, J.: A medical panorama: the casebooks project. Book 2.0 **4**(1–2), 61–69 (2014)
14. Ingram, D.: The good european health record. In: Laires, M.F., Ladeira, M.F., Christensen, J.P. (eds.) Health in the New Communication Age, pp. 66–74. IOS (1995)
15. Isern, D., Moreno, A.: Computer-based execution of clinical guidelines: a review. Int. J. Med. Inform. **77**(12), 787–808 (2008)
16. Isern, D., Sánchez, D., Moreno, A.: Ontology-driven execution of clinical guidelines. Comput. Meth. Programs Biomed. **107**(2), 122–139 (2012)
17. Kalra, D., Lewalle, P., Rector, A., Rodrigues, J.M., Stroetmann, K.A., Surjan, G., Ustun, B., Virtanen, M., Zanstra, P.E.: Semantic interoperability for better health and safer healthcare. Research and Deployment Roadmap for Europe. SemanticHEALTH Project Report, Published by the European Commission (2009). http://ec.europa.eu/information_society/ehealth
18. Martínez-Costa, C., Menárguez-Tortosa, M., Fernández-Breis, J.T., Maldonado, J.A.: A model-driven approach for representing clinical archetypes for semantic web environments. J. Biomed. Inform. **42**(1), 150–164 (2009)
19. Menárguez-Tortosa, M., Fernández-Breis, J.T.: Owl-based reasoning methods for validating archetypes. J. Biomed. Inform. **46**(2), 304–317 (2013)
20. Montero, M.A., Prado, S.: Electronic health record as a knowledge management tool in the scope of health. In: Riaño, D. (ed.) K4HelP 2008. LNCS (LNAI), vol. 5626, pp. 152–166. Springer, Heidelberg (2009). doi:10.1007/978-3-642-03262-2_12
21. Mosa, A.S.M., Yoo, I., Sheets, L.: A systematic review of healthcare applications for smartphones. BMC Med. Inform. Decis. Making **12**(1), 1 (2012)
22. Musen, M.A., Middleton, B., Greenes, R.A.: Clinical decision-support systems. In: Shortliffe, E.H., Cimino, J.J. (eds.) Biomedical Informatics, pp. 643–674. Springer, New York (2014)
23. Ohno-Machado, L., Gennari, J.H., Murphy, S.N., Jain, N.L., Tu, S.W., Oliver, D.E., Pattison-Gordon, E., Greenes, R.A., Shortliffe, E.H., Barnett, G.O.: The guideline interchange format. J. Am. Med. Inform. Assoc. **5**(4), 357–372 (1998)
24. Peleg, M.: Computer-interpretable clinical guidelines: a methodological review. J. Biomed. inform. **46**(4), 744–763 (2013)
25. Quesada-Martínez, M., Fernández-Breis, J.T., Karlsson, D.: Suggesting missing relations in biomedical ontologies based on lexical regularities. Stud. Health Technol. Inform. **228**, 384 (2016)
26. Quesada-Martínez, M., Fernández-Breis, J.T., Stevens, R.: Lexical characterization and analysis of the BioPortal ontologies. In: Peek, N., Marín Morales, R., Peleg, M. (eds.) AIME 2013. LNCS (LNAI), vol. 7885, pp. 206–215. Springer, Heidelberg (2013). doi:10.1007/978-3-642-38326-7_31
27. Quesada-Martínez, M., Fernández-Breis, J.T., Stevens, R.: Lexical characterisation of bio-ontologies by the inspection of regularities in labels. Curr. Bioinform. **10**(2), 165–176 (2015)
28. Rector, A., Iannone, L.: Lexically suggest, logically define: quality assurance of the use of qualifiers and expected results of post-coordination in snomed ct. J. Biomed. Inform. **45**(2), 199–209 (2012)

29. Rector, A.L., Johnson, P.D., Tu, S., Wroe, C., Rogers, J.: Interface of inference models with concept and medical record models. In: Quaglini, S., Barahona, P., Andreassen, S. (eds.) AIME 2001. LNCS (LNAI), vol. 2101, pp. 314–323. Springer, Heidelberg (2001). doi:10.1007/3-540-48229-6_43

30. Schober, D., Tudose, I., Svatek, V., Boeker, M.: Ontocheck: verifying ontology naming conventions and metadata completeness in protégé 4. J. Biomed. Semant. **3**(2), 1 (2012)

31. Shahar, Y., Young, O., Shalom, E., Galperin, M., Mayaffit, A., Moskovitch, R., Hessing, A.: A framework for a distributed, hybrid, multiple-ontology clinical-guideline library, and automated guideline-support tools. J. Biomed. Inform. **37**(5), 325–344 (2004)

32. Sherman, R.: Computer system clears up errors, lets nurses get back to nursing: a progress report from children's hospital, Akron, Ohio. Hosp. Top. **43**(10), 44–46 (1965)

33. Smith, B., Ashburner, M., Rosse, C., Bard, J., Bug, W., Ceusters, W., Goldberg, L.J., Eilbeck, K., Ireland, A., Mungall, C.J., et al.: The obo foundry: coordinated evolution of ontologies to support biomedical data integration. Nature Biotechnol. **25**(11), 1251–1255 (2007)

34. Tao, C., Jiang, G., Oniki, T.A., Freimuth, R.R., Zhu, Q., Sharma, D., Pathak, J., Huff, S.M., Chute, C.G.: A semantic-web oriented representation of the clinical element model for secondary use of electronic health records data. J. Am. Med. Inform. Assoc. **20**(3), 554–562 (2013)

35. Third, A.: Hidden semantics: what can we learn from the names in an ontology? In: Proceedings of the Seventh International Natural Language Generation Conference, pp. 67–75. Association for Computational Linguistics (2012)

36. Tu, S.W., Eriksson, H., Gennari, J.H., Shahar, Y., Musen, M.A.: Ontology-based configuration of problem-solving methods and generation of knowledge-acquisition tools: application of protege-ii to protocol-based decision support. Artif. Intell. Med. **7**(3), 257–289 (1995)

37. Warner, H.R., Toronto, A.F., Veasey, L.G., Stephenson, R.: A mathematical approach to medical diagnosis: application to congenital heart disease. Jama **177**(3), 177–183 (1961)

38. Wilk, S., Michalowski, W., Michalowski, M., Farion, K., Hing, M.M., Mohapatra, S.: Mitigation of adverse interactions in pairs of clinical practice guidelines using constraint logic programming. J. Biomed. Inform. **46**(2), 341–353 (2013)

39. Wright, A., Sittig, D.F.: A four-phase model of the evolution of clinical decision support architectures. Int. J. Med. Inform. **77**(10), 641–649 (2008)

40. Yao, W., Kumar, A.: Conflexflow: Integrating flexible clinical pathways into clinical decision support systems using context and rules. Decis. Support Syst. **55**(2), 499–515 (2013)

Clinical Quality, Evaluation, and Simulation

Formalization and Computation of Diabetes Quality Indicators with Patient Data from a Chinese Hospital

Haitong Liu[1], Annette ten Teije[2], Kathrin Dentler[2(✉)], Jingdong Ma[1], and Shijing Zhang[1]

[1] Department of Medicine and Health Management,
Huazhong University of Science and Technology, Wuhan, China
liuhaitong1991@gmail.com
[2] Department of Computer Science, VU University Amsterdam,
Amsterdam, The Netherlands
{annette.ten.teije,k.dentler}@vu.nl

Abstract. Clinical quality indicators are tools to measure the quality of healthcare and can be classified into structure-related, process-related and outcome-related indicators. The objective of this study is to investigate whether Electronic Medical Record (EMR) data from a Chinese diabetes specialty hospital can be used for the automated computation of a set of 38 diabetes quality indicators, especially process-related indicators. The clinical quality indicator formalization (CLIF) method and tool and SNOMED CT were adopted to formalize diabetes indicators into executable queries. The formalized indicators were run on the patient data to test the feasibility of their automated computation. In this study, we successfully formalized and computed 32 of 38 quality indicators based on the EMR data. The results indicate that the data from our Chinese EMR can be used for the formalization and computation of most diabetes indicators, but that it can be improved to support the computation of more indicators.

Keywords: Diabetes mellitus · Clinical quality · Quality indicators · Electronic medical record · Formalization · Secondary use of patient data

1 Introduction

Clinical quality indicators are tools to evaluate the quality of healthcare services and the performance of hospitals. The most widely adopted classification system for quality indicators has been proposed by Donabedian [1]. In his classification, indicators are distinguished into structure-related, process-related and outcome-related indicators. Structure denotes the attributes of the settings in which care occurs, process denotes what is actually done in giving and receiving care and outcome denotes the effects of care on the health status of patients and populations.

© Springer International Publishing AG 2017
D. Riaño et al. (Eds.): KR4HC/ProHealth 2016, LNAI 10096, pp. 23–35, 2017.
DOI: 10.1007/978-3-319-55014-5_2

In the background of China's health reform, healthcare quality is affected by the implementation of different health policies, such as the reconstruction of healthcare organizations and workflow improvements, the adjustment of the reimbursement strategy and the innovation of diagnosis and treatment techniques. Therefore, the assessment of healthcare quality is drawing much attention. In China, clinical indicators released by the government are widely adopted among hospitals. These indicators usually aim at the overall quality of a hospital and are mainly structure-related and outcome-related indicators, which are used to assess performance and rate hospitals.

In 2011, Dentler [2] proposed a method to formalize clinical quality indicators. The CLIF method consists of 9 steps to formalize any clinical indicator into a computer-interpretable query. Based on this method, Dentler [3,4] also developed the clinical quality indicator formalization tool which was adopted to formalize 159 quality indicators to be computed on Dutch patient data. The diabetes quality indicators that we use in this study are a subset of these 159 indicators. Our aim for this study is to assess the feasibility of the formalization and computation of diabetes indicators based on Chinese patient data. This enables us to learn about the reproducibility of the formalization of the diabetes indicators and the generalisability and (re-)usability of the CLIF method and tool in a culturally, technically and medically different environment.

2   Materials and Methods

2.1   Quality Indicators

As Chinese clinical indicators are mostly structure-related and outcome-related with a lack of process-related indicators, we use the same diabetes indicator set as used in Dentler's research [2], which has been released by the Dutch Healthcare Inspectorate in 2011. The indicator set contains 38 indicators in total, of which 23 are process-related, 10 are outcome-related and the other 5 are demographic indicators. The indicators involve many aspects of diabetes patients such as the diagnosis, laboratory tests and treatments. A list of the indicators can be seen in Table 1.

2.2   Patient Data

We use patient data from the EMR system of the Qingdao Endocrine and Diabetes Hospital in China. The EMR adopted in the hospital is consistent with the Chinese EMR data standard [5], which is adopted by many hospitals in China. For our study, we selected only diabetes patients (major diagnosis or secondary diagnosis). The data set ranges from the year 2010 to the year 2014 and contains 9,094 patients in total. For our computation, we used only patient data of 2013 and 2014, as it was more complete and of higher quality, it included 1,866 patients in total. The original data set is divided into 5 different tables: the diagnosis table, the patient table which mainly contains the admission records,

Table 1. Set of diabetes indicators. All indicators are for patients with an age below 80.

ID	Definition	Type
I1	Known diabetes patients in the practice population at the end of the reporting period	(demographic)
I2	Type 1 diabetes patients of all known diabetes patients in the practice population at the end of the reporting period	(demographic)
I3	Type 2 diabetes patients of all known in the practice population at the end of the reporting period	(demographic)
I4	Diabetes patients who are treated in primary care in the practice population at the end of the reporting period	(demographic)
I5	Diabetes patients who are treated in primary care and are enrolled for 12 months or longer at the end of the reporting period	(demographic)
I6	Diabetes patients whose HbA1c has been determined in the last 12 months	process
I8	Diabetes patients with HbA1c below 53 mmol/mol (<53)	outcome
I10	Diabetes patients with HbA1c above 69 mmol/mol (>69)	outcome
I11	Diabetes patients whose blood pressure has been determined in the past 12 months	process
I13	Diabetes patients with systolic blood pressure of 140 mmHg or lower (≤140)	outcome
I16	Diabetes patients whose lipid profile (total cholesterol and triglycerides and HDL and LDL) has been determined	process
I17	Diabetes patients with total cholesterol value of less than 4.5 mmol/L (<4.5)	outcome
I18	Diabetes patients with LDL-cholesterol value of less than 2.5 mmol/L (<2.5)	outcome
I19	Diabetes patients using a lipid-lowering drug (e.g. statins)	process
I20	Diabetes patients whose eGFR was calculated or determined in the past 12 months	process
I23	Diabetes patients with eGFR between 60 ml/min (<60) and 30 (≥30)	outcome
I24	Diabetes patients with eGFR less than 30 ml/min (<30)	outcome
I25	Diabetes patients with urinalysis (portions) of albumin or albumin/creatinine ratio in the past 12 months	process
I27	Diabetes patients whose smoking status was known	process
I28	Patients who smoke in the group of patients whose smoking status was known	process
I30	Patients who received over the past 12 months advice to quit smoking in the group of patients who smoke	process

(continued)

Table 1. (*continued*)

ID	Definition	Type
I31	Diabetes patients whose body mass index has been calculated (known) in the last 12 months	process
I33	Diabetes patients whose body mass index less than 25 (<25)	outcome
I36	Diabetes patients whose diet has been discussed in the past 12 months	process
I37	Diabetes patients whose alcohol consumption has been registered in the last five years	process
I38	Diabetes patients whose physical activity levels has been recorded in the past 12 months	process
I39	Diabetes patients with foot examination in the past 12 months	process
I40	Diabetes patients with a record of Simm's classification of foot examination	process
I41	Patients with diabetic foot abnormalities (abnormal findings at last check)	outcome
I42	Diabetes patients with fundus check in the past 24 months	process
I43	Diabetes patients with diabetic retinopathy	outcome
I44	Patients with only non-medication treatment (lifestyle and/or diet)	process
I45	Patients medically treated only with oral antidiabetics	process
I46	Patients treated medically with oral antidiabetics and insulin	process
I47	Patients medically treated only with insulin	process
I48	Patients diagnosed with DM-2 and BMI $\geq$ 25 who are prescribed metformin (denominator: patients with DM-2 and BMI $\geq$ 25)	process
I49	Patients vaccinated against influenza in the previous 12 months	process
I50	Patients with the combination of data on the aforementioned process indicators (HbA1c, blood pressure, lipid profile, kidney function, smoking status, BMI, foot examinations and eye examinations)	process

the laboratory test table, the physical examination/imaging table and the treatment table. We applied the following processing: (1) Deleted irrelevant data fields from the tables (for example occupation, address, insurance). (2) Annotated the fields with SNOMED CT codes in every table except the "patient" table. For the diagnosis table, the SNOMED CT to ICD-10 mappings from the IHTSDO were used to automatically map the ICD-10 diagnosis codes to SNOMED CT codes. For the other three tables, the mappings were conducted manually. The database schema can be seen in Fig. 1 (omitting some date fields). (3) In the "patient" table, the personal history is stored in the form of text which contains

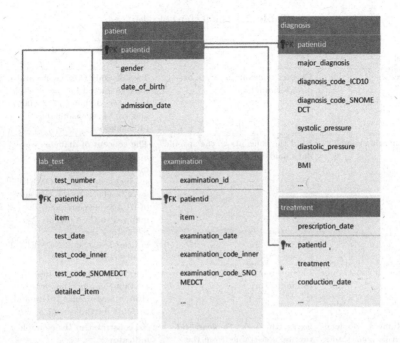

Fig. 1. The database schema of the patients database

the smoking history, drinking history and injury history. We used a small natural language processing program to extract the information about smoking history and inserted a structured data field to represent the smoking history. The NLP program has previously been validated with sample data from this study and demonstrated a precision of 97% and recall rate of 65%.

2.3 CLIF Tool

The main idea behind the CLIF method is to divide the formalization of clinical quality indicators into 9 steps [2]. The CLIF tool implements the method to guide a user through the formalization process to represent a quality indicator as an executable database query. All steps together with an example based on indicator I6 (HbA1c measured) are detailed in Table 2.

The CLIF tool is programmed in PHP and can be connected to a local database to formalize indicators and compute their results. We modified the original CLIF tool to suit this study in the following ways: (1) we adjusted the character encoding to fit the requirements of processing Chinese characters; (2) we adjusted the database connection to fit the data structure of the patient database; (3) we translated the user interface to Chinese; and (4) we modified some datatypes to suit the Chinese patient data. Both the modified CLIF tool and its source code are publicly available[1].

---

[1] http://cliftool.org/, https://github.com/LiuHaitong/CLIF2.

Table 2. The 9 steps of CLIF

Step	Definition	An example based on indicator I6
1. Concepts	Extract relevant concepts based on a terminology	Two SNOMED CT concepts were extracted for the example indicator: diabetes (73211009) and HbA1c measurement (43396009)
2. Information model	Bind the concepts to the specific data fields of the patient data	The concept of diabetes was mapped to the table of diagnosis as diagnosis.diagnosis_code_SNOMEDCT = 73211009, and the concept of HbA1c measurement was mapped to the table of laboratory test as lab_test.test_code_SNOMEDCT = 43396009
3. Temporal constraints	Extract temporal constraints from the indicator	The temporal constraints contain the reporting year, HbA1c measurement date and patients' birthday (age < 80)
4.–6. Numeric, Boolean and textual constraints	Extract numeric, Boolean and textual constraints from the indicator	No constraint in the example indicator
7. Grouping of constraints	Group and combine the constraints with Boolean connectors	All constraints were connected by "AND"
8. Exclusion criteria	Identify the exclusion criteria from the constrains defined in previous steps	No constraint was an exclusion criterion
9. Numerator	Identify the constraints which only aim at the numerator	Laboratory test code and HbA1c measurement date

2.4　Evaluation

We adopted three different methods to evaluate our results. Firstly, the computed results were analyzed based on widely adopted Chinese clinical guidelines to check whether there were obviously erroneous results. Subsequently, the computed results were compared to Dentler's original results based on Dutch patient data to analyze their correlation. Finally, we conducted an expert review with an endocrinologist to assess the accuracy of the computed results. We informed the endocrinologist about the source of the patient data and about the definitions of each indicator. We then provided him with the computed results and asked him to judge by his clinical experience whether the results are accurate or not. We then discussed the possible causes of seemingly inaccurate results.

3 Results

3.1 Formalization of the Indicators

All indicators can be formalized based on an arbitrary structure of the patient database. However, based on the real patient data structure, 6 of our 38 indicators can not be formalized completely, namely I5, I30, I36 to I38 and I40. Of these indicators, I5 involve the enrollment of patients, while the EMR did not have a corresponding data field to store this information. I30 is about the patients who received advice to quit smoking. This kind of information can not be classified as laboratory test or examination and there is no specific data field in the patient table to store this information in the EMR. Therefore, the formalization stopped at step 2 (definition of the information model). Similar problems occurred for indicator I36 (diet discussion of the patients), I37 (alcohol consumption registration), I38 (physical activity levels recording) and I40 (recording of Simm's classification of foot examination).

SNOMED CT Concepts Used. In Dentler's study, different coding systems were adopted to represent the concepts, such as the International Classification of Primary Care (ICPC) for diagnosis-related concepts, Anatomical Therapeutic Chemical (ATC) for medication-related concepts and a Dutch national coding system for laboratory concepts. In the current study, only SNOMED CT codes were used to represent all the concepts of diagnosis, laboratory test, examination and treatment. The diagnosis concepts in the patient data were mapped automatically from ICD-10 codes and other concepts were mapped manually from internal codes of the hospital or from text. A summary of the concepts used in this study is shown in Table 3. An advantage of SNOMED CT is that it can be used to "bridge" concepts that occur in the patient data and typically higher-level concepts that occur in indicators via its subclass hierarchy.

Table 3. Number of SNOMED CT concepts used in this study

Category	In patient data	In formalized indicators
diagnosis-related	110	3
laboratory test-related	48	4
examination-related	17	3
treatment-related	187	6
other	0	2

Although using different coding systems (SNOMED CT versus ICPC, ATC, Dutch Laboratory ontology), this experiment shows the reproducibility of the formalization of the diabetes quality indicators.

3.2   Computed Results of the Indicators

All formalized indicators were run via the CLIF tool to compute their results. Based on the patient data of 2013 and 2014, some indicators return no patient, which may be due to absent data or because there is indeed no patient satisfying the indicator. Figure 2 shows a comparison of the results of 2013 and 2014. The results represent the percentage of patients who satisfy the respective indicators, most of the which were similar.

Applying the CLIF approach on Chinese data shows us the generalisability of CLIF. The same method and tool work in a culturally, technically and medically different environment.

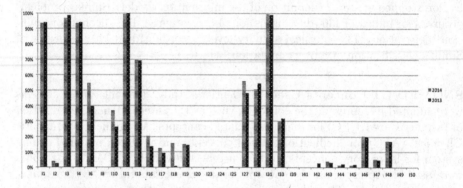

Fig. 2. A comparison of the computed results of 2013 and 2014

3.3   Analysis and Evaluation of the Results

An analysis based on guidelines

Even though Chinese hospitals implement different clinical guidelines for the management of diabetes patients, there are still some widely adopted guidelines in Chinese hospitals [6]. Based on these, we can interpret the computed results and the clinical quality. The following analysis is mainly based on the data of 2014.

(1) HbA1c measurement.

In Chinese hospitals it is recommended to measure the HbA1c of all admitted patients as it reflects the seriousness of the patients' condition during admission. However, the main treatment plan is developed based on the value of blood glucose, not the HbA1c. The computed results of I6 (patients with measured HbA1c) indicated that only 54% of the patients had HbA1c measured in 2014, which indicates unsatisfactory quality. For all the patients with HbA1c measured, no patient had a value of <53 mmol/L (I8) while 68% of the patients had a value of >69 mmol/L (I10/I6), which may mean that HbA1c is only measured for patients in a serious condition.

(2) Lipids profile measurement.
Chinese guidelines recommend to measure the lipids profile for all patients and the core goal of lipids control is to lower the LDL cholesterol level to less than 2.6 mmol/L. The computed results indicated that most patients' blood cholesterol is well controlled, for example, in 2014, 94 of the 151 patients whose lipids profile has been measured had a total cholesterol <4.5 mmol/L (I17/I16) and 117 of 151 patients whose lipids profile has been measured had a LDL cholesterol <2.5 mmol/L (I18/I16). This may also be the reason why few patients were prescribed lipid-lowering drugs (I19).

(3) Other laboratory tests.
The three indicators about the calculation of estimated glomerular filtration rate (eGFR) (I20, I23, I24) return no patient, as the calculation of eGFR is usually not recorded in Chinese EMRs. Urinalysis is not a required measurement based on Chinese guidelines, and the urinalysis indicator (I25) confirms that urinalysis was performed only for few patients.

(4) Examinations indicators.
The computed results indicated that no patient received foot examination or fundus check and only a small percentage of patients have been recorded with foot or eye complications, which may not reflect the reality. As the authors know, the examinations of foot and eye are common for diabetes patients in Chinese hospitals but these examinations are usually not recorded in the EMR.

(5) Treatment indicators.
The treatment indicators classify the treatment into non-medication treatment, insulin treatment and oral anti-diabetic drugs. 467 patients of 2013 and 346 patients of 2014 were recorded with treatment. A small percentage of the patients was treated only with non-medication treatment, only insulin and only oral anti-diabetic drugs. In Chinese guidelines, insulin is recommended to be adopted when non-medication treatments are not adequate to achieve the blood glucose control goal. Also, insulin is recommended to be used in combination with oral anti-diabetic drugs to improve the therapeutic effects and avoid adverse effects of insulin-only treatment, such as hypoglycemia and body weight gain. The computed results indicate that most of the patients with recorded treatment data were prescribed insulin plus oral anti-diabetic drugs, which is in accordance with the guidelines.

Comparison with Dentler's results
We analyzed the correlation of the computed indicator results of this study with Dentler's results, and found that they were not correlated. This might be due to the fact that the data in Dentler's study stemmed from a primary context, whereas this study used data from a hospital, which treats patients in more

serious conditions. Besides, Chinese hospitals and Dutch hospitals may adopt different clinical guidelines, which also may contribute to the differences between the results.

Expert review

The expert detected some computed results which were obviously lower than expected, including for foot examination (I39), fundus examination (I42) and eGFR calculation (I20, I23, I24). According to the expert's experience, these examinations are very common among diabetes patients during their admission to hospitals, but the procedures are usually not recorded in the EMR, which may be the reason why these indicators appeared lower.

The expert also considered that patients treated with anti-diabetic drugs seemed lower than expected (I45, I46, I47). After a detailed analysis of the treatment data, we found that many patients were treated with Chinese traditional medicine. This was recorded in the EMR, but is not classified as oral anti-diabetic drugs, insulin or lifestyle adjustment in SNOMED CT, which lowered the result. According to the expert, the remaining results were reasonable.

4   Related Work

Ontologies are important tools in the field of knowledge representation (KR). The adoption of ontologies for the representation of clinical indicators is highly related to the representation of clinical guidelines [7]. Clinical guidelines and clinical quality indicators have much in common, for example they all involve the measurement of physiological data and time-sensitive data. Therefore, early research about the formalization of indicators focused on the mining of common features of different indicators and the construction of indicator ontologies. Beyan [8] constructed an indicator ontology to model clinical indicators, based on which he developed an indicator search system. Surján [9] developed an indicator ontology based on the 19 public health indicators released by WHO, which improved the comparability of different indicators to some degree. The studies above all constructed indicator ontologies, which focused on the modeling of different dimensions of quality indicators and were used to enable convenient retrieval from indicator databases. In contrast, Dentler's [2] study focused on the formalization of the indicators' content, such as the extraction of concepts and relations, which were used for the computation of indicators.

Early research about the automated computation of clinical indicators mainly focused on the automated collection of patient data and the specific algorithm, which emphasized the construction of information systems (such as EMRs) and the database technology. For example, Newland [10] adopted the database management system of Stockert to achieve the automated computation of clinical quality indicators of cardiopulmonary by-pass surgery. Shabot [11] implemented a clinical information system in Cedars-Sinai medical center to collect the ICU patient data and compute 6 ICU core indicators published by the Joint Commission on Accreditation of Healthcare Organizations (JCAHO) of the US.

In recent years, more researchers began to pay attention to the handling of unstructured data, especially in the format of text. Baldwin [12,13] developed a natural language processing (NLP) tool to extract concepts from clinical narratives. Mehrotra [14] tried to extract usable information from colonoscopy reports by NLP methods to enable the computation of clinical indicators. Garvin [15] adopted NLP methods to construct regular expressions to extract ejection fraction from unstructured data to support the computation of clinical indicators related to heart failure. Brown [16,17] developed the SNOMED-CT based eQuality system to extract concepts from text to support the computation of indicators. The system is validated to achieve the precision of 96% and recall of 86%. However, the eQuality mainly aimed at the quality measurement of disability examinations records, and did not focus on the quality of medical services.

5   Discussion

The EMR patient data is acute disease-oriented. The EMR is suitable for the collection and storage of acute disease data, not the information about chronic care. For example, the examination of the patients stored in the table of examination are mostly about imaging. Therefore, the query to retrieve patients with diabetic foot examinations and fundus checks does not return any result. Also, the treatment data mainly recorded the medication and surgeries of the patients and does not contain details about lifestyle therapy and exercise.

Besides, we found a lack in data standards. In most Chinese hospitals, diagnoses are coded with ICD-10, and surgery procedures are coded with ICD-9, while other data fields such as lab test and physical examination are usually coded by internal hospital codes or not coded at all. The internal codes are usually coarse and it is not possible to represent the relations between different codes. This impedes the computation of some indicators, especially process-related indicators.

The EMR data quality also influenced the accuracy of the computed results, especially missing and erroneous data. For example, the foot examination and eye examination data are both not recorded in the EMR, which leads to the fact that the computation of corresponding indicators does not return any patient.

To better support the computation of clinical indicators based on EMRs, some measures must be implemented to improve the EMR structure and data quality. An effective way is to adopt more terminology codes or data standards. The adoption of formal terminology codes such as SNOMED CT or data coding standards are both ways to improve the computability of clinical quality indicators. It will reduce the cost of manual transformation and increase the accuracy of the computed results. Medical ontologies are better than data standards as they contain the relationships of different concepts and are suitable for the computation of process-related indicators.

Another way is to increase the degree of structured information in the EMR. Chinese EMR data contains unstructured free text, making it hard to compute the indicators. For example, we used an NLP method to extract information regarding the smoking history from the free-text field of personal history, which furthermore includes the drinking history and injury history. Storing such information in structured data fields would be an effective way to improve the feasibility of computing clinical quality indicators.

Finally, the CLIF tool could be improved. For example, step 6 of the CLIF method is to "formalize textual constraints", but the CLIF tool only implements a rather basic functionality. To integrate the CLIF tool with NLP tools would be beneficial. Also, the encoding of concepts could be (semi-)automated by using automated annotation tools.

6   Conclusion

In this study, the CLIF method and tool were used to formalize 38 diabetes indicators, and the formalized queries were run on collected EMR data of diabetes patients to test the feasibility of their automated computation. Our results show that, based on the Chinese hospital EMR data structure, 32 of the 38 indicators can be computed successfully, 18 of which are process-related indicators. Most of the non-computable indicators are process-related. This shows the generalisability of the CLIF method in a completely different environment (China versus The Netherlands). A three-fold evaluation highlighted some areas for improvement.

7   Future Work

Because there are no widely adopted diabetes quality indicators in the Chinese context, especially when it comes to process-related indicators, we used Dutch quality indicators in this study. Future studies may investigate the definition of clinical quality indicators based on Chinese evidence-based materials, such as clinical guidelines, and test the feasibility of computing these Chinese indicators.

References

1. Donabedian, A.: The quality of care: how can it be assessed? Jama **260**(12), 1743–1748 (1988)
2. Dentler, K., Numans, M.E., ten Teije, A., et al.: Formalization and computation of quality measures based on electronic medical records. J. Am. Med. Inform. Assoc. **21**(2), 285–291 (2014)
3. Dentler, K., Cornet, R., ten Teije, A., et al.: The reproducibility of CLIF, a method for clinical quality indicator formalisation. In: MIE, pp. 113–117 (2012)
4. Dentler, K., Cornet, R., ten Teije, A., et al.: Influence of data quality on computed Dutch hospital quality indicators: a case study in colorectal cancer surgery. BMC Med. Inf. Decis. Making **14**(1), 1 (2014)

5. Xu, W., Guan, Z., Cao, H., et al.: Analysis and evaluation of the Electronic Health Record standard in China: a comparison with the American national standard ASTM E 1384. Int. J. Med. Inf. **80**(8), 555–561 (2011)
6. Weng, J.: Evolution in the Chinese diabetes society standards of care for type 2 diabetes. Diab. Metab. Res. Rev. **32**(5), 440–441 (2016)
7. White, P., Roudsari A.V.: From computer-interpretable guidelines to computer-interpretable quality indicators: a case for an ontology. In: ICIMTH, pp. 99–102 (2014)
8. Beyan, O.D., Baykal, N.: A knowledge based search tool for performance measures in health care systems. J. Med. Syst. **36**(1), 201–221 (2012)
9. Surján, G., Szilágyi, É., Kováts, T.: A pilot ontological model of public health indicators. Comput. Biol. Med. **36**(7), 802–816 (2006)
10. Newland, R.F., Baker, R.A., Stanley, R.: Electronic data processing: the pathway to automated quality control of cardiopulmonary bypass. J. Extra Corporeal Technol. **38**(2), 139 (2006)
11. Shabot, M.M.: Automated data acquisition and scoring for JCAHO ICU core measures. In: AMIA (2005)
12. Baldwin, K.B.: Evaluating quality of primary care using the electronic medical record. J. Healthc. Qual. **28**(6), 40–47 (2006)
13. Baldwin, K.B.: Evaluating healthcare quality using natural language processing. J. Healthc. Qual. **30**(4), 24–29 (2008)
14. Mehrotra, A., Dellon, E.S., Schoen, R.E., et al.: Applying a natural language processing tool to electronic health records to assess performance on colonoscopy quality measures. Gastrointest. Endosc. **75**(6), 1233–1239 (2012)
15. Garvin, J.H., DuVall, S.L., South, B.R., et al.: Automated extraction of ejection fraction for quality measurement using regular expressions in Unstructured Information Management Architecture (UIMA) for heart failure. J. Am. Med. Inf. Assoc. **19**(5), 859–866 (2012)
16. Brown, S.H., Elkin, P.L., Rosenbloom, S.T., et al.: eQuality for all: extending automated quality measurement of free text clinical narratives. In: AMIA Annual Symposium Proceedings, vol. 2008, p. 71. American Medical Informatics Association (2008)
17. Brown, S.H., Speroff, T., Fielstein, E.M., et al.: eQuality: electronic quality assessment from narrative clinical reports. In: Mayo Clinic Proceedings, vol. 81, no. 11, pp. 1472–1481 (2006)

Simulation-Based Episodes of Care Data Synthetization for Chronic Disease Patients

David Riaño[✉] and Alberto Fernández-Pérez

Research Group on Artificial Intelligence, Universitat Rovira i Virgili, Tarragona, Spain
david.riano@urv.cat

Abstract. Primary care studies related to chronic diseases and their treatment use to be based on the analysis of large amounts of episodes of care (EoC) in order to check standard's compliance, improve protocols, or perform quality and cost studies. In these EoC, data related to the patient condition and treatment are registered along the different encounters between the patient and the health care professionals. However, EoC data analysis is subject to some limitations such as data availability, reliability, and appropriateness, aside of multiple legal issues. Several studies exist to surpass these limitations with software technologies that synthesize realistic clinical data. Two are the main approaches: data-driven, or the construction of quantitative models from data about retrospective clinical cases, and knowledge-driven, or the construction of qualitative (semantic) models from the accumulation of medical evidences.

These approaches have some limitations that we aimed to surpass with a computer-based virtual-patient simulation system to synthesize EoC data for chronic diseases that have been applied to generate data about long-term treatment of hypertension cases. Unlike other previous systems, our approach takes advantage of the pros of both, the data- and the knowledge-driven approaches. In this paper we introduce the system, apply it to produce EoC synthetic data about virtual patients with arterial hypertension, and identify a limited number of modifiers of the system that allow adaptation and, therefore, the progressive improvement of the synthesized data generated.

Keywords: Clinical data synthetization · Patient modeling · Patient simulation

1 Introduction

Clinical data analysis is an important work area of medical research. However, the availability of such data is not always straightforward due to several complications such as availability, privacy, awareness, scarcity, appropriateness, etc. Moreover, clinical data is highly sensitive and therefore framed in a legal setting (either local, national, or international) that hampers its use in research, arguably to protect patient privacy and hospital proprietary concerns [1–4]. The obvious value of this sort of data in the advance of research has also been noticed by health care centers and health care systems and institutions that have started to offer clinical databases such as GPRD (www.gprd.com), QRESEARCH (www.qresearch.org), THIN (www.thin-uk.com), PHARMO (www.pharmo.nl), or SIDIAP (www.sidiap.org) for

© Springer International Publishing AG 2017
D. Riaño et al. (Eds.): KR4HC/ProHealth 2016, LNAI 10096, pp. 36–50, 2017.
DOI: 10.1007/978-3-319-55014-5_3

secondary use (i.e., research). But, the access to these data still requires some protective measures (e.g., anonymization, selection, etc.), proprietary arrangements, usage rights, and costs to consider, this causing some nuisances to the stakeholders.

The need of data, on one hand, and the issues accessing these data, on the other hand, both describe a reality that research has to cope with. Some researchers consider computer synthetization of realistic clinical data a technological solution to have quality data available whilst getting rid of those collateral annoyances [1–6]. So, Moniz et al. [3] state that using synthetic data eliminates all disclosure risks completely; Buczak et al. [4] indicate that data synthetization allows creating background records and artificial outbreaks or emergencies that are not present (or hard to find) in the real data, and contribute to the standardization of test data; Huang et al. [6] consider that synthetized data improve availability (direct use without approval), publicity (data can be made publicly available), complementarity (synthetic data can avoid biases, inconsistencies and missing, erroneous, and noisy values), rarity (synthetic data is not constrained by case prevalence), and typicality (data synthetization can be used to generate benchmarks).

There are not many antecedents on clinical data synthetization [5] and the ones found can be classified into data-driven [1–4], knowledge-driven [6], and patient simulation [9]. Data driven approaches are mainly quantitative and they use prior databases as the baseline to generate new synthetic data. Internal database correlations, frequencies, conditional probabilities, or data associations are used to generate the new data. Knowledge-driven approaches, which tend to be qualitative, use available knowledge-bases as constraints to generate new data that must not contradict the clinical knowledge in these knowledge-bases. Far less evident, in medical education, the concept of patient simulation or virtual patient refers to the (computer) modelling of a patient in order to train medical students. The information derived from the interactions between a realistic patient model and health care professionals can also be the source to generate synthetic data [7, 10].

Current data-driven approaches such as [1–4] have been criticized based on their dependency on (1) data availability, (2) a trustworthy anonymization procedure, and (3) the possible implementation of inverse methods to re-identify real cases [5]. Knowledge-driven solutions [6] have other issues: (1) knowledge availability and completeness, (2) knowledge fragmentation and granularity, and (3) incremental production of a correct representation of knowledge.

In health care, chronic patients have a particular long-time representation of data which is based on the clinical concept called Episode of Care (EoC). An EoC is described as a sequence of encounters of a patient and the health care professionals attending her from admission to discharge about one particular health problem, each encounter recording the date of the encounter, the current condition of the patient, and the treatment prescribed.

In this paper, we present the engineering process of making a knowledge-based computer architecture to synthesize EoC data for chronic diseases. The process is founded on (1) the construction of a patient simulation model or virtual patient whose clinical signs evolve as new encounters of the EoC are synthesized; (2) a limited number of statistical evidences that can be obtained from clinical archives; and (3) some basic medical knowledge that is computerized from clinical practice guidelines or expert physicians. The architecture is being tested to synthesize EoC data about the long-term treatment of arterial hypertension (virtual) patients.

This paper is organized as it follows: Sect. 2 describes the components of the data synthesizer. Section 3 exposes the application of this synthesizer to generate EoCs for hypertension. In Sect. 4 we discuss about the achievements, and propose ideas for future work.

2   Methods

Figure 1 depicts the general architecture of the knowledge-based system that we have used to synthesize EoC data about patients suffering from a chronic condition. It comprises three levels: the (medical) *Knowledge Level* containing background medical information related to the chronic disease to consider, the *Simulation Level* containing the structures required to simulate a chronic patient, and the *Synthetization Level* containing the computer libraries for EoC data generation.

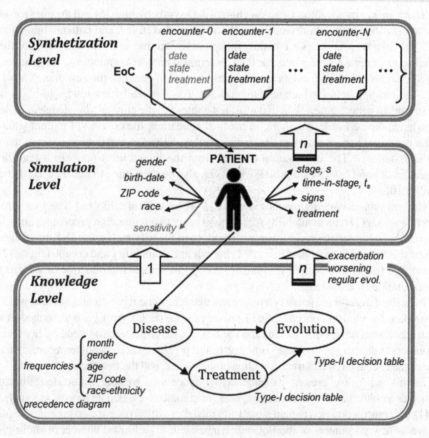

Fig. 1.   The 3-level system architecture

2.1   The Medical Knowledge Level

The whole system for EoC data synthetization is based on concrete units of medical knowledge. These units of knowledge contain the core information which determines how data is going to be generated. Basically, this information can be classified into statistical information and guideline and expert information.

Statistical information is obtained from retrospective data about the EoC contained in the information systems of health care centers (e.g., the centers of the health care group SAGESSA [18, 19]).

Guideline and expert information is a kind of knowledge contained in clinical practice guidelines and clinical pathways that experts can help us to interpret before it is incorporated in the EoC data synthesizer.

In our system, we have grouped medical knowledge into disease knowledge, treatment knowledge, and evolution knowledge, as Fig. 1 depicts. Arrows represent knowledge dependencies. So, the treatment knowledge depends on the disease considered (e.g., hypertension is treated with a hypertension therapy), and the evolution of the patient depends on both the diagnosed disease and the treatment applied (e.g., the evolution of a patient with hypertension depends on the patient's stage of the disease and other parameters, but also on her concrete treatment of hypertension).

Disease Knowledge.   Statistical information related to the frequency of cases per *month* of the year (January to December), per *gender* (male or female), per *age* of the patient (or age intervals), per *ZIP code*, and per *race-ethnicity* (White, Black, Asian, Latino, or Middle East) is registered for the target disease. These statistical parameters are used to determine the distribution of cases with regard to each attribute, having no impact in the evolution of the disease. This information can be obtained from Health Care administration or local health care centers' databases.

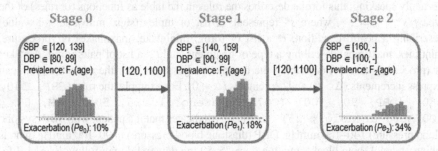

Fig. 2. Stage precedence diagram for Hypertension.

Chronic diseases evolve along *stages* that can represent levels of severity, usually deserving different treatments. These stages and their evolutions define a *precedence diagram* that can be depicted as a graph with vertices standing for disease stages, and edges indicating the evolutions between pairs of stages. See a simplified example in Fig. 2 where nodes contain: (1) a description of the patients in the stage as [min, max] constraints of the values of a selected number of signs; (2) a distribution function of the prevalence of patients per age, for each single stage; and (3) an exacerbation risk as a percentage of patients suffering an exacerbation while in the stage. Edges contain a time interval defining the [mintime, maxtime] values for a regular patient to evolve from one stage to the next stage. Time is considered to be a key factor to determine the evolution of the disease because patient worsening is a typical characteristic of chronic diseases, as time passes.

All the information related to the prevalence of patients in one stage, the exacerbation risks, the changes of stage (i.e., edges), and the evolution time intervals between edges can be calculated from the past cases registered in the archives of primary care services, while the patient description in the stages uses to be found in the clinical guidelines of the target disease.

Note that the simplified precedence diagram in Fig. 2 represents the natural evolution of the disease from milder to more severe stages. But this evolution is not necessarily unidirectional. Along a patient evolution, the signs can also improve as a consequence of the medical treatment and therefore the patient may reach a stable condition in her current stage or even move to a better stage of the disease.

The Treatment Knowledge. Clinical practice guidelines contain therapeutic indications that Clinical Pathways adapt to concrete clinical contexts. These indications can be defined at different levels of granularity (e.g., the Anatomical Therapeutic Chemical Classification (ATC) defines five levels of detail for drugs, the ATC Defined Daily Doses (DDD) describes the average dose per day for drugs in adults, and the ICD-10-PCS provides a classification of medical procedures in seven abstraction levels).

Decision tables are knowledge representation structures that have been previously used to describe clinical procedures [8, 11, 15, 16]. They are understandable, manageable, and easy to computerize, and can adopt different formats [8, 11, 14]. Here, we take the format presented in [8] in order to represent the medical treatment knowledge of our system. Formally speaking, this format describes the rules in the table as functions (or rules) of the type $f_i(s^*, t^*) = t'^*$, where s^* represents a list of tuples (sign, minvalue, maxvalue) describing a health condition,. t^* a list of (drug, minintake, maxintake) or (procedure, mintimes, maxtimes) describing a type of treatment, and t'^* a list of pairs (drug, Δintake) or (procedure, Δtimes) describing the treatment adjustment after the encounter, that can express increments ($\Delta > 0$) and decrements ($\Delta < 0$). For example, the rule (SBP, 140, 160) (DBP, 90, 100) (C07AB03-atenolol, 25, 50) (LSM, 0) → (C07AB03-atenolol, 25) (LSM, 1) indicates that if a patient with SBP (systolic blood pressure) 140–160 mmHg, DBP (diastolic blood pressure) in 90–100 mmHg, who is taking atenolol (beta-blocker) with a dose 25–50 mg/day and do not follow a LSM (lifestyle modification program), must increase the dose of the beta-blocker in 25 mg/day, and start the LSM.

This format has been validated in different clinical research settings [11–13]. Figure 3 describes part of the treatment knowledge introduced in the type-I decision table of our system. Columns represent the s^*'s, rows the t^*'s, and cells the t'^*'s. In this representation, granularity is at the drug level; with drug being one among thiazide derivatives (ATC code C02DA), beta-blocking agents (C07A), ACE inhibitors (C09A), ARB blockers (C09CA), or calcium channel blockers (C08G).

TYPE-I DT	BP <= 120/80	BP > 120/80 BP<=140/90	BP > 140/90 BP<=160/100	BP > 160/100
- Null treatment	- Recommend LSM	- Recommend LSM - Prescribe 1 drug	- Recommend LSM - Prescribe 1 drug	- Recommend LSM - Prescribe 1 drug
- Following a good lifestyle	- Recommend LSM	- Recommend LSM - Prescribe 1 drug	- Recommend LSM - Prescribe 1 drug	- Recommend LSM - Prescribe 1 drug
- Taking 1 drug	- Keep taking 1 drug	- Increase dosage	- Increase dosage	- Increase dosage
- Taking 1 drug (max dosage)	- Keep taking 1 drug (max dosage)	- Add 2nd drug (min dosage)	- Add 2nd drug (min dosage)	- Add 2nd drug (min dosage)
- Taking 1 drug - 2nd drug added	- Keep taking 2 drugs	- Replace 2nd drug	- Replace 2nd drug	- Replace 2nd drug
- Taking 1 drug - 2nd drug replaced	- Keep taking 2 drugs	- Add 3rd drug	- Add 3rd drug	- Add 3rd drug
- Taking 2 drugs	- Keep taking 2 drugs	- Add 3rd drug (min dosage)	- Add 3rd drug (min dosage)	- Add 3rd drug (min dosage)
- Taking 2 drugs - 3rd drug added	- Keep taking 3 drugs	- Replace 3rd drug	- Replace 3rd drug	- Replace 3rd drug
- Taking 2 drugs - 3rd drug replaced	- Keep taking 3 drugs	- Keep taking 3 drugs - Go to specialist	- Keep taking 3 drugs - Go to specialist	- Keep taking 3 drugs - Go to specialist
- Taking 3 drugs	- Keep taking 3 drugs	- Keep taking 3 drugs - Go to specialist	- Keep taking 3 drugs - Go to specialist	- Keep taking 3 drugs - Go to specialist

Fig. 3. Part of type-I decision table for Hypertension defined at primary care.

The Evolution Model. Whenever a patient with a health condition receives a treatment, this treatment is expected to make the patient to remain in a stable condition or to evolve to a new (better) condition, after a time. Our system simulates three sorts of evolutions: exacerbation, worsening, and regular evolution. *Exacerbation* is considered an unexpected acute worsening of the patient condition that requires an urgent intervention. *Worsening* is the natural evolution of a chronic disease from a previous milder stage to the next more serious stage where the patient is expected to stay. *Regular evolution* is the normal consequence of the treatment delivered to a patient and it may require follow-up.

The probability of exacerbation (Pe_s) of a patient with a health condition in a stage s is registered in the corresponding stage of the precedence diagram (see Fig. 2). A random percentage p is used to determine whether the next evolution of the patient is an exacerbation ($p \leq Pe(s)$), or not ($p > Pe(s)$). If exacerbation is discarded, the range of evolution [mintime, maxtime] between the current stage and the following stage in the precedence diagram, and the time t_s the patient has been in the current stage are used to determine if a worsening occurs. A new random percentage p' is used to find the value v, such that Eq. 1 is satisfied. If $t_s > v$, a patient condition worsening is simulated, otherwise a regular evolution of the patient is accepted.

$$\frac{v - mintime}{maxtime - mintime} > \frac{p' - 10}{90} \tag{1}$$

Exacerbations can last for several encounters (e.g., 1–3) and they imply the sudden serious worsening of one or more signs of the patient (soft exacerbations imply 10–25%

of signs deterioration, whilst hard exacerbations imply >25% of signs deterioration). Worsening entails a change of stage, and therefore an evolution of the signs of the virtual patient to the values of these signs in the new stage. Finally, patient regular evolutions are the result of applying a type-II decision table to the current patient condition and treatment.

Type-II decision tables can be found in previous works such as [7, 8, 11]. They implement patient evolutions as functions (or rules) of the type $f_{II}(s^*, t^*) = s'^*$, where s^* represents a list of tuples (sign, minvalue, maxvalue) describing a sort of patient condition, t^* is a list of (drug, minintake, maxintake) or (procedure, mintimes, maxtimes) describing a sort of treatment, and s'^* a list of pairs (sign, Δvalue) describing the patient health condition adjustment after the treatment t^* takes effect. For example, the rule (SBP, 140, 160) (DBP, 90, 100) (C07AB03-atenolol, 25, 50) → (SBP, 10) (DBP, 5) means that the SBP/DBP of patients with a SBP/DBP 140-160/90-100 mmHg may increase 10/5 mmHg after taking atenolol 25–50 mg/day.

Figure 4 shows the knowledge contained in the type-II decision table which is used to simulate the evolution of patients that are in the health condition s^* expressed in the columns, when they are subject to the treatment t^* expressed in the rows. The regular evolutions s'^* of some of the signs are expressed in the table cells as mild/moderate/high increments ($\Delta > 0$) or decrements ($\Delta < 0$), or no change ($\Delta = 0$).

TYPE-II DT	BP > 120/80 BP<=140/90	BP > 140/90 BP<=160/100	BP > 160/100
- Null treatment	- BP mild increment	- BP moderate incr.	
- Following LSM	- BP mild increment	- BP mild increment	
- Taking 1 drug	- BP mild decrement	- BP mild decrement	- BP high decrement
- Taking 1 drug (max dosage)	- BP mild decrement	- BP moderate decr.	- BP high decrement
- Taking 1 drug - 2nd drug added	- BP mild decrement	- BP moderate decr.	- BP moderate decr.
- Taking 1 drug - 2nd drug replaced	- BP moderate decr.	- BP mild decrement	- BP mild decrement
- Taking 2 drugs	- BP moderate decr.	- BP mild decrement	- BP moderate decr.
- Taking 2 drugs - 3rd drug added	- BP moderate decr.	- BP moderate decr.	- BP high decrement
- Taking 2 drugs - 3rd drug replaced	- BP moderate decr.	- BP mild decrement	- BP high decrement
- Taking 3 drugs	- BP moderate decr.	- BP mild decrement	- BP high decrement

Fig. 4. Type-II decision table for Hypertension defined at primary care.

2.2   The Patient Simulation Level

The central component of the EoC data synthesizer implements a virtual patient affected by the target disease. The data structure of this patient is composed of *static information* (i.e., gender, birth-date, ZIP-code, race-ethnicity, and sensitivity), and *dynamic information* (i.e., stage, time-in-stage, signs, and treatment). Static information is fixed during the creation of the virtual patient, and their values remain unchanged for the whole EoC data synthetization process of this patient. Statistical information about the disease in the Knowledge Level is used to determine whether the patient is male or female (gender), his/her birth-date (mm-dd-yyyy), ZIP-code, and race-ethnicity (i.e., White, Black, Asian, Latino, Middle East).

Patient's sensitivity is a table showing the sensitivities and resistances to concrete clinical drugs [13]. So, a 100% sensitivity means normal sensitivity (i.e., standard DDD doses should be prescribed), <100% sensitivities means drug resistance (i.e., augmented DDD doses are expected), and >100% drug hypersensitivity (i.e., reduced DDD doses are recommended) [7]. See, for example, in Fig. 5 the case of an elder patient who is resistant to beta-blockers and hypersensitive to ARB-blockers.

	Sort	Sensitivity
C02DA thiazide derivatives	drug	100%
C07A Beta-blocking agents	drug	80%
C09A ACE inhibitors	drug	100%
C09CA ARB blockers	drug	105%
C08G calcium channel blockers	drug	100%

Fig. 5.   Sensitivities of a virtual patient to drugs for hypertension.

If this patient has a BP = 150/100 mm Hg, and takes a beta-blocker at normal dose, the table in Fig. 4 would prognosticate a mild decrement of the BP (e.g., 140/90), but since the patient is 80% resistant to beta-blockers, the BP reduction would cause BP to be 142/92 mm Hg.

In our system, patient simulation is based on the patient's dynamic information change as the virtual patient evolves as a result of the treatment. The system registers the current stage of the virtual patient among the ones contained in the precedence diagram of the disease (see Fig. 2), and accumulates the total time the patient has remained in this stage. This information is used to assess whether the patient can or cannot evolve to a new stage as an effect of an exacerbation, a worsening, or a regular evolution as it was discussed in the previous section. Broadly speaking, there are two main actions on the virtual patient: generation and evolution.

Virtual Patient Generation. New patients can be generated from the information contained in the Knowledge Level. Once a disease is fixed, a virtual patient suffering from this disease is generated. First, we calculate the static information from the disease knowledge (i.e., gender, birth-date, ZIP-code, and race-ethnicity), then a random process determines the sensitivity table of the patient to all the possible drugs (e.g., 80% of the sensitivities are 100%, 20% of them are resistances, and 20% hypersensitivities). In a second step, the age of the patient is used to determine his/her stage among the ones in the stage precedence diagram of the disease. The prevalence distribution functions are used for that. Once the initial stage is determined, the initial patient condition (i.e., signs and values) is calculated. All the signs contained in the stage description are copied with values in the corresponding [min, max] intervals. Other signs not contained in the definition of the stage are assigned normal values. Time in stage is set to zero, and the current treatment is null. At this point the virtual patient is ready to synthesize the data corresponding to the admission encounter.

Virtual Patient Evolution. Every time a new encounter has to be synthesized, the virtual patient is evolved. Evolution consists in the application to the type-I decision table to the current condition and treatment of the patient. Observe that the current treatment can be null, the first time, but this can be managed by the table (see Fig. 3). The treatment suggested by the table is then stored as the current treatment of the virtual patient, and a new encounter can be synthesized. After synthetization, the type-II table is applied to calculate the evolution of the current signs of the virtual patient from the current signs and the stored treatment. This evolution is modified according to the virtual patient sensitivities in the sensitivity table, and the resulting values stored as the new condition of the virtual patient. The virtual patient is then ready for a new evolution unless a discharge condition is detected. The current system implements two sorts of discharge: *exitus* and *time-out*. Exitus happens when the values of some of the signs of the patient reach extreme values and the virtual patient is considered to die. Time-out is when the virtual patient reaches a date that is beyond the limit of dates of the EoC data that we want to synthesize (e.g., if we want to generate episodes ending in the year 2015).

In the current study, we have not considered other sorts of EoC closures different from exitus or time-out because our purpose is to synthesize full EoCs. However, the system is designed to allow easy incorporation of additional follow-up interruptions such as patient withdrawal, patient shift to specialized treatments, patient hospitalizations, patient health care urgencies, etc.

2.3   The Episode of Care Data Synthetization Level

Once a virtual patient is defined according to the procedure previously described, an Episode of Care (EoC) can be made reflecting the evolution of that patient along the treatment from its admission to a final discharge: *exitus* or *time-out*. In the EoC, the encounters are composed of a date (or moment when the encounter takes place), a state (or condition of the patient during the encounter), and a treatment (or set of drugs prescribed and procedures performed during the encounter). Outlined in Fig. 1, our procedure to synthesize EoC data makes a distinction between the first encounter of the EoC (i.e., encounter-0 or admission) and the following encounters.

Synthesizing the first encounter. It is made in two steps. During the first step the date of the encounter is synthesized by selecting (1) a month according to the prevalence of cases per month, (2) one year in the interval [former-year, later-year][1] provided as input parameters of the system, and (3) a random day among the correct days in that month and year. Then, the state of the encounter is copied from the state of the virtual patient. In a second step, the information in the state is used to determine the appropriate treatment suggested by the decision table type-I. The recommended treatment is copied in both, the virtual patient dynamic information, and the current EoC encounter.

Synthesizing subsequent encounters. Patients evolve by means of exacerbations, worsenings, or regular evolutions, as it was explained in Sect. 2.1. Any of the three alternatives provide a time increment Δt (in number of days) that allows the patient to evolve to the next treatment step. In order to assess the evolution of this patient after this time, the former patient health condition (group of signs) and treatment (group of drugs and clinical actions) are considered by the type-II decision table to infer the current health condition of the patient, also expressed as a group of valued signs. This new description of the patient condition replaces the previous condition of the virtual patient, and a new encounter is generated. The process to generate this next encounter is in three steps: firstly, calculating the new date adding Δt to the date of the former encounter. Secondly, copying the signs of the virtual patient as signs of the encounter, and finally, recalculating the treatment in the encounter with the type-I decision table.

Closing the EoC. Basically, there are two ways to automatically stop the generation of encounters in an EoC. When the system detects that the health condition of the virtual patient is not possible because one or more signs are out of a living range, the patient is considered to die (*exitus*). Also, when the patient evolves to a time that surpasses the terminal date limit that we want for the generated episodes, the EoC is also closed (*time-out*).

Note that the purpose of our work is to synthesize EoC data rather than to generate health care full records. EoCs can be seen as a simplification of patient records where only the information about the evolution of the patient and the treatment at specific moments (i.e., encounters) are registered.

3   Synthesizing EoC Data of Patients with Hypertension

The clinical practice guideline [17], the information system of SAGESSA (www.grupsagessa.com) with regard to the treatment of real hypertensive patients, and our experience and computer-interpretable knowledge on past projects [11, 13, 18–20] are the source of information used to implement the three levels of our EoC data synthesizer for arterial hypertension. This information and the results are exposed in the next subsections.

---

[1] The value later-year determines the EoC *time-out* termination.

3.1   Prevalent Information

Retrospective data in SAGESSA was used to extract patient frequencies related to gender, ages, and race-ethnicity. The time intervals to evolve among stages (i.e., worsenings) was also determined from the data, but adjusted according to the criterion of clinical experts. For this purpose, we used the accumulated data in SAGESSA during the years 2011, 2012, and 2013, corresponding to 9271 patients with arterial hypertension alone. Similarly, the time between consecutive encounters was fixed to be in the interval [3 weeks, 4 months] after a first analysis from the observed values in the data, and a later refinement by the experts. However, exacerbations can occur at a shorter time than 3 weeks.

3.2   Decision Tables

The knowledge contained in our type-I decision table was taken from [13]. This knowledge had been tested with a system to manage chronic comorbid patients [12]. Once converted, this knowledge gave rise to a decision table with rules whose antecedent could contain two signs (i.e., SBP and DBP), one action (i.e., LSM), and three prescriptions (i.e., take 1, 2, or three drugs among thiazide derivatives, beta-blocking agents, ACE inhibitors, ARB blockers, and calcium channel blockers). Rule consequents could prescribe two actions (i.e., LSM and visit specialist), and six drug intake modifiers per drug (i.e., introduce drug, replace drug, cancel drug, and prescribe low, intermediate, or high doses). We got 7 rules for normal stage -1 (i.e., $BP \leq 120/80$), 16 rules for stage 0 (i.e., $120/80 < BP \leq 140/90$), 14 rules for stage 1 (i.e., $140/90 < BP \leq 160/100$), and 16 rules for stage 2 (i.e., $BP > 160/100$).

Type-II decision table was made to contain the knowledge that we isolated from the regular evolutions detected in the SAGESSA data. A long expert-supported preprocessing of this knowledge was required to obtain the rules in Fig. 4. Further improvements of the contents of this table is not discarded and left for future work. This knowledge was transformed into the rules of our type-II decision table that, for concrete patient BPs and treatments, the evolution of BP values could be predicted. These evolutions could be null, mild, moderate, or high, with respective increments 0/0, [0,10]/[0,5], [10, 15]/[5, 7], or [15, 20]/[7, 10] mmHg for SBP/DBP. The final number of rules in our type-II decision table was 53.

3.3   Generating Episodes of Care

The EoC data synthesizer was used to generate long term treatment information for twenty virtual patients whose sample description (age, gender, ethnicity, etc.) is shown in Table 1. The selected period was 1/1/2013, 12/31/2015.

Most of the patients (85%) arrived in advanced stages, 1 and 2, with an average BP 154/99 mmHg. Evolution through consecutive EoC encounters were simulated, and related data synthesized: most of the evolutions (54%) were single increments of stage that required assistance. Among the 9 encounters representing severe worsening (12%), 6 were due to exacerbation (among 13 exacerbation encounters in total). Interestingly, the treatment and evolution knowledge contained in type-I and type-II decision tables was able to stabilize patients 60% of times in average. Exacerbations were controlled in 3 visits or less (5 exacerbations in 1 visit).

Table 1. Sample description of the twenty virtual patients and treatments generated.

Patient (N = 20)
Static information
    Age (first encounter): 69.75 ± 9.83
    Gender: female (55%), male (45%)
    Ethnicity: white (10%), black (15%), asian (20%), latino (30%), middle east (25%)
Dynamic information and Patient evolution
    Stage (first encounter):–1 (15%), 0 (20%), 1 (45%), 2 (40%)
    Signs (first encounter): SBP (154 ± 26 mmHg), DBP (99 ± 19 mmHg)
Evolution
    Stage no. of changes and magnitude (± X: increase/decrease X stages)
    Total: +1 (40–54%), +2 (9–12%), −1 (11–15%),−2 (13 – 18%)
    Due to exacerbation and related emergency action: +2 (6), −2 (10)
Sort of evolution
    % worsenings-improvements-stabilizations btw consecutive episodes:19% - 21% - 60%
    No. exacerbated patients:7
    No. exacerbations and duration in No. of encounters: 1 enc (5), 2 enc (3), 3 enc (5).
    No. exacerbations per exacerbated patient:1.43 ± 0.53
    Severity of exacerbation: SBP (49.00 ± 24.91), DBP (29.62± 25.40)

Treatment
    Days in treatment per patient: 458.70 ± 283.51
Encounters
    No. encounters per patient: 11.15 ± 8.24
    Stages (total):–1 (66 enc), 0 (67 enc), 1 (41 enc), 2 (49 enc)
    Days between consecutive encounters: 69.10 ± 90.03
Drugs
    No patients with pharmacological treatment: 17 (2/4/11 patients with 1/2/3 drugs)
    No. drugs/encounter:0 drug (6 enc), 1 drug (52 enc), 2 drug (41 enc), 3 drug (123 enc)
    No encounters with pharmacological treatment:1 drug (52), 2 drug (41), 3 drug (123)
Visits to specialist
    No. visits: 16 (6 because exacerbations)
No. visits per patients visiting: 0 visits (10), 1 visit (5), 2 visits (4), 3 visits (1)

The average treatment takes 458.7 days and 11.15 encounters[2], among which 60% were mild conditions (stages −1 and 0), and 40% severe conditions (stages 1 and 2). Eleven patients deserved 3-drug treatment at some point of the treatment, and only 2 were controlled with one single drug. Only six encounters did not require pharmacological treatment, and 16 a derivation to the specialist, 6 of them due to uncontrolled exacerbations.

---

[2] Chronic diseases last for long periods, so treatment duration depends on the study time interval mainly and it should not be interpreted as the average curing time.

The evolution of the SBP for the first ten patients is depicted in Fig. 6. P2 and P7 were patients with one severe exacerbation that could be controlled after 2 episodes, and then progressively re-conducted to their original SBP values. P6 was a very unstable patient with two extreme exacerbations in one year. P3's SBP gets stable (below 120 mmHg) after an initial adjustment of the treatment. P4 arrives at the end of the period with a high SBP which the provided treatment is able to lower to reasonable values after two visits. P8 is a patient that after two visits remains with a high SBP, requiring further treatment improvement after the selected period of study.

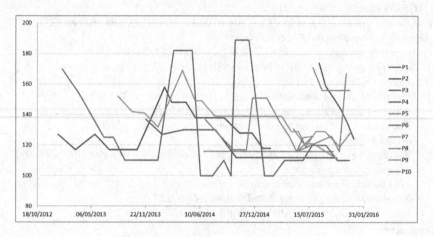

Fig. 6. Ten first patients BP evolutions.

4   Discussion, Conclusions, and Future Work

Some of the problems related to accessing clinical data can be avoided with the use of synthesized data. Two main technological approaches exist to synthesize clinical data as clinical records, but they have been criticized and some limitations exposed. In order to overcome these problems we developed a virtual patient simulation-based system for EoC data synthetization and used it to generate arterial hypertension long-term EoC-like treatments and patient evolutions. It is founded on a limited amount of information resources that we have identified as epidemiological statistical information and guideline and expert information.

Statistical information: the system requires (1) frequencies of cases per month, gender, age ranges (5-year blocks), and race-ethnicity; (2) distribution functions of prevalence of patients per age and exacerbation risk percentage in each stage of the precedence diagram; (3) evolutions and [mintime, maxtime] intervals in the precedence diagram, and (4) a type-II decision table describing the expected evolution of one patient under a concrete condition and treatment. All this information can be obtained from retrospective data contained in the information systems of health care centers.

Guideline and expert information: the system uses (1) the disease stages in the precedence diagram, defined in term of signs and [min max] value ranges, and (2) a type-I decision table describing what treatment to provide to each situation described by a current patient condition and treatment. All this information is contained in clinical practice guidelines and clinical pathways that the experts can help us to interpret.

Moreover our system has three internal decision points that can be tuned to adjust the results and to synthesize more realistic data. These are: (1) decide when an evolution is an exacerbation, a worsening, or a regular evolution; (2) decide the duration of exacerbations in terms of number of encounters, and (3) decide the sensitivity of patients to drugs.

The current results are promising, however further work is required in order to be able to synthesize fully realistic data. At the moment, we are working with a GP in order to identify unrealistic behaviors (i.e., weird evolutions and treatments). Our current version is acceptable, according to the GP, but still may be improved in terms of the time delays between encounters and virtual patient evolutions, and the effects of the treatment (i.e., type-II table). Our final validation will consist on testing the quality of our data by three means: (1) confronted to real patient data with the use of EoC similarity metrics still to be defined, (2) making physicians not to distinguish between real and synthesized EoCs after a random presentation of cases, (3) plotting real and synthesized data together and checking that their distribution is undistinguishable, and (4) using clustering methods separately on the synthesized data, and on the real data and analyzing equivalences between the classes obtained.

Problem dimensionality will also be reconsidered. So, some other parameters which are not currently used, such as family antecedents, lifestyle issues (e.g., smoking, alcohol intake, or dietary habits), etc. will be considered in future extensions of the system.

We also aim to apply our system to other chronic and critical diseases and to synthesize EoC data about multimorbid virtual patients.

References

1. Buczak, A.L., Moniz, L.J., Copeland, J., et al.: Data-driven hybrid method for synthetic electronic medical records generation. In: Proceedings of the IDAMAP 2008, pp. 81–86 (2008)
2. Buczak, A.L., Moniz, L.J., Feighner, B.H., Lombardo, J.S.: Mining electronic medical records for patient care patterns. In: Proceedings of the IEEE Symposium CIDM 2009, pp. 146–153 (2009)
3. Moniz, L., Buczak, A.L., Hung, L., et al.: Constuction and validation of synthetic electronic medical records. Online J. Public Health Inform. 1(1), e2 (2009)
4. Buczac, A.L., Babin, S., Moniz, L.: Data-driven approach for creating synthetic electronic medical records. Med. Inform. Decis. Making 10, 59 (2010)
5. Dube, K., Gallagher, T.: Approach and method for generating realistic synthetic electronic healthcare records for secondary use. In: Gibbons, J., MacCaull, W. (eds.) FHIES 2013. LNCS, vol. 8315, pp. 69–86. Springer, Heidelberg (2014). doi:10.1007/978-3-642-53956-5_6
6. Huang, Z., Harmelen, F., Teije, A., Dentler, K.: Knowledge-based patient data generation. In: Riaño, D., Lenz, R., Miksch, S., Peleg, M., Reichert, M., Teije, A. (eds.) KR4HC/ProHealth 2013. LNCS (LNAI), vol. 8268, pp. 83–96. Springer, Heidelberg (2013). doi:10.1007/978-3-319-03916-9_7

7. Real, F., Riaño, D., Alonso, J.R.: A patient simulation model based on decision tables for emergency shocks. In: Riaño, D., Lenz, R., Miksch, S., Peleg, M., Reichert, M., Teije, A. (eds.) KR4HC 2015. LNCS (LNAI), vol. 9485, pp. 21–33. Springer, Heidelberg (2015). doi:10.1007/978-3-319-26585-8_2

8. Riaño, D.: A systematic analysis of medical decisions: how to store knowledge and experience in decision tables. In: Riaño, D., Teije, A., Miksch, S. (eds.) KR4HC 2011. LNCS (LNAI), vol. 6924, pp. 23–36. Springer, Heidelberg (2012). doi:10.1007/978-3-642-27697-2_2

9. Talbot, T.B., Sagae, K., John, B., Rizzo, A.A.: Sorting out the virtual patient. Int. J. Gaming Comput. Mediated Simul. **4**(3), 1–19 (2012)

10. Real, F., Riaño, D., Alonso, J.R.: Training residents in the application of clinical guidelines for differential diagnosis of the most frequent causes of arterial hypertension with decision tables. In: Miksch, S., Riaño, D., Teije, A. (eds.) KR4HC 2014. LNCS (LNAI), vol. 8903, pp. 147–159. Springer, Heidelberg (2014). doi:10.1007/978-3-319-13281-5_11

11. Real, F.: Use of decision tables to model assistance knowledge to train medical residents. Universitat Rovira i Virgili. Ph.D. dissertation (2016)

12. Riaño, D., Collado, A.: Model-based combination of treatments for the management of chronic comorbid patients. In: Peek, N., Marín Morales, R., Peleg, M. (eds.) AIME 2013. LNCS (LNAI), vol. 7885, pp. 11–16. Springer, Heidelberg (2013). doi:10.1007/978-3-642-38326-7_2

13. Chowdhury HMS. CDML: A Chronic Disease Management. MSc dissertation (2013)

14. Shiffman, R.N.: Representation of clinical practice guidelines in conventional and augmented decision tables. J. Am. Med. Inform. Assoc. **4**(5), 382–393 (1997)

15. Shiffman, R.N., Greenes, R.A.: Use of augmented decision tables to convert probabilistic data into clinical algorithms for the diagnosis of appendicitis. In: Proceedings of the Annual Symposium on Computer Application in Medical Care, pp. 686–690 (1991)

16. Bielza, C., Pozo, Juan, A.,Fernández, Lucas, P.: Finding and explaining optimal treatments. In: Dojat, M., Keravnou, Elpida, T., Barahona, P. (eds.) AIME 2003. LNCS (LNAI), vol. 2780, pp. 299–303. Springer, Heidelberg (2003). doi:10.1007/978-3-540-39907-0_41

17. Chobanian, A.V., et al.: The seventh report of the joint national committee on prevention, detection, evaluation, and treatment of high blood pressure (2003)

18. Bohada, J.A.: Automatic production and integration of knowledge to the support of the decision and planning activities in medical-clinical diagnosis, treatment and prognosis. Ph.D. dissertation (2012)

19. López-Vallverdú, J.A.: Knowledge-based incremental induction of clinical algorithms. Ph.D. dissertation (2012)

20. Riaño, D., Real, F., et al.: An ontology-based personalization of health-care knowledge to support clinical decisions for chronically ill patients. JBI **45**(3), 429–446 (2012)

A Public Health Surveillance Platform Exploiting Free-Text Sources via Natural Language Processing and Linked Data: Application in Adverse Drug Reaction Signal Detection Using PubMed and Twitter

Pantelis Natsiavas[1,2(✉)], Nicos Maglaveras[1,2], and Vassilis Koutkias[1,2]

[1] Lab of Computing and Medical Informatics, Department of Medicine,
Aristotle University of Thessaloniki, Thessaloniki, Greece
{pnatsiavas,nicmag}@med.auth.gr
[2] Institute of Applied Biosciences, Centre for Research and Technology Hellas,
Thermi, Thessaloniki, Greece
vkoutkias@certh.gr

Abstract. This paper presents a platform enabling the systematic exploitation of diverse, free-text data sources for public health surveillance applications. The platform relies on Natural Language Processing (NLP) and a micro-services architecture, utilizing Linked Data as a data representational formalism. In order to perform NLP in an extendable and modular fashion, the proposed platform employs the Apache Unstructured Information Management Architecture (UIMA) and semantically annotates the results through a newly developed UIMA Semantic Common Analysis Structure Consumer (SCC). The SCC output is a graph represented in the Resource Description Framework (RDF) based on the W3C Web Annotation Data Model (WADM) and SNOMED-CT. We also present the use of the proposed platform through an exemplar application scenario concerning the detection of adverse drug reaction (ADR) signals using data retrieved from PubMed and Twitter.

Keywords: Public health surveillance · Micro-services · Semantic Web · Linked Data · Natural Language Processing · Adverse drug reactions

1 Introduction

The biggest data source of our times, the World Wide Web (WWW) and the various services on top of that contain and constantly generate vast amounts of unstructured data which could be exploited in the context of biomedical research. The term "unstructured data" refers broadly to data that do not follow a predefined data model or format to facilitate the analysis purpose. Frequently, the term is used to refer at large amounts of free-text and multimedia content which is accompanied with little or no metadata related with the target analysis as it has been created to serve other purposes (e.g. content publishing, everyday communication, decision auditing, etc.). However, this kind of data potentially contain further information that can be systematically exploited in the

© Springer International Publishing AG 2017
D. Riaño et al. (Eds.): KR4HC/ProHealth 2016, LNAI 10096, pp. 51–67, 2017.
DOI: 10.1007/978-3-319-55014-5_4

context of the target analysis scenario. For example, free-text content is largely present in Electronic Health Records (EHRs), in terms of clinical narratives, which could be exploited for adverse drug events detection. Similarly, bibliographic databases and even social media content have also been exploited for adverse drug event detection [1]. In general, mining such free-text sources brings many challenges as well as new opportunities for information extraction and knowledge discovery.

In this paper, we present a software platform enabling the systematic exploitation of free-text sources through Natural Language Processing (NLP), aiming to support public health surveillance applications. The proposed platform satisfies the following three main requirements:

1. Interoperability with other systems in terms of standards-based data linking and reuse, independently of the respective analytic processes;
2. Semantic annotation of NLP results that would facilitate further analysis, or reuse of widely accepted knowledge sources;
3. Reusability of the developed software modules, in order to support alternative application workflows within the platform.

In the current paper, we mainly focus on the following two key design aspects of the platform:

1. Knowledge representation which has been addressed by adopting Linked Data principles [2], and
2. the use of the micro-services paradigm [3], as the main architecture pattern.

The term Linked Data refers to a group of technologies and standards which facilitate the interconnection and the joint exploitation of data. The micro-services architectural paradigm dictates modelling the various system components as functionally and technically autonomous "services" which can be developed, maintained and scaled independently.

Major emphasis in the paper is also given on the Semantic Common Analysis Structure Consumer (SCC), a module that we developed on top of the Apache Unstructured Information Management Architecture (UIMA) [4]. UIMA is an open-source platform used to analyze unstructured data and NLP is one of its typical uses in a wide range of applications[1]. SCC is developed as one of the core platform modules, used to semantically annotate the results of the UIMA NLP analysis, using Linked Data formalisms, in order to facilitate interoperability and allow semantic processing of the produced outcome (e.g. via automatic inference using reasoning software).

As a proof-of-concept application, we elaborate on the detection of adverse drug reaction (ADR) signals by exploiting social media and bibliographic databases [1, 5], namely, PubMed[2] and Twitter[3]. According to the Council for International Organizations of Medical Sciences (CIOMS) VIII Working Group [6], signals in the domain of

---

[1] https://www.ibm.com/blogs/research/2011/04/open-architecture-helps-watson-understand-natural-language/.

[2] https://www.ncbi.nlm.nih.gov/pubmed/.

[3] https://twitter.com/?lang=en.

pharmacovigilance are defined as *"information that arises from one or multiple sources (including observations and experiments), which suggests a new potentially causal association, or a new aspect of a known association, between an intervention and an event or set of related events, either adverse or beneficial, that is judged to be of sufficient likelihood to justify verificatory action"*. In the scope of this work, we focus on adverse events. We selected this use case due to its complexity and high impact, while the interest in using the above sources originates from their vast amount of data and their dynamic nature, since these are populated with new content constantly.

The paper is structured as follows: In Sect. 2, we refer to related works focusing on public health surveillance platforms and the use of technologies adopted in the current work. In Sect. 3, we present the main platform modules and our key design decisions, while in Sect. 4, we provide details as regards platform implementation and present the proof-of-concept application on ADR signal detection. Finally, in Sect. 5, we discuss the key platform design decisions based on our experiences through the proof-of-concept application, as well as limitations of the current work and future work plans.

2   Related Work

The need to establish comprehensive IT frameworks for public health surveillance has been illustrated through recent exemplar initiatives such as Query Health [7], and ARTEMIS [8]. Query Health defines a-standards-based approach for distributed population health queries through a national architecture exploiting diverse clinical system data models. ARTEMIS focuses on antimicrobial resistance through a Semantic Web based architecture fostering the integration and interoperability of inter-institutional and cross-border microbiology laboratory databases. Furthermore, several platforms focusing on public health scenarios using NLP and Linked Data technologies have been proposed. In particular, eDRUGS [9] and GRITS [10] exploit social media to extract information regarding specific aspects of public health (use of cannabinoids and epidemiological information). Moreover, an early warning system regarding ADRs exploiting web sources (i.e. forums) is presented in [11], while the PREDOSE platform [12] provides social media analytics regarding drug abuse epidemiology based on Semantic Web technologies.

The specific data sources used in the presented platform, namely PubMed and Twitter, have been both used for public health surveillance applications. Shang et al. exploited recently PubMed data to identify plausible ADRs [13], while Twitter has been extensively used for various applications, including drug safety surveillance [14], H1N1 outbreak monitoring [15], prediction of asthma-related emergency department visits [16], and identification of allergy associations [17]. Besides Twitter, other social media platforms, e.g. Facebook [18] and YouTube [19] have also been exploited for public health surveillance. Interestingly, various studies pursued the exploitation of multiple, diverse sources for public health surveillance in parallel with social media, e.g. Google search logs and Twitter trends for respiratory syndrome correlations [20], trends and posts from social media platforms, hospital visits and self-reporting to improve influenza surveillance [21], as well as PubMed data, Twitter posts and spontaneous reports from FDA for drug safety surveillance [22].

Regarding the platform's two key design points, Linked Data have been used to face the challenges imposed by the Extract-Transform-Load (ETL) processes in big data public health surveillance scenarios [23]. Furthermore, Linked Data have been used in social media knowledge extraction processes [12, 24] by semantically annotating data to facilitate integration and analysis using domain knowledge formed in ontologies. Moreover, the micro-services architectural paradigm has been employed in Internet of Things (IoT) applications (e.g. [25, 26]), as well as in biomedical informatics related platforms (e.g. [27]).

3   Methods

In this section, we present the design of the proposed platform focusing on the two key design decisions, i.e. the use of Linked Data as the platform's data representational format and the micro-services architectural paradigm.

3.1   Data Sources

The free-text data sources elaborated until now in our platform are PubMed and Twitter. PubMed is the reference bibliographic source in the domain of health and life sciences, which is continuously updated with new scientific articles. Twitter is a social media micro-blogging service used by hundreds of million people every day.

PubMed can be considered as a "big growing lake" of free-text data, as it is a huge medical research paper repository, which is constantly growing. Its content is considered rather credible, as it has been peer-reviewed as part of the pre-publication procedure. On the other hand, Twitter can be considered as a an unlimited number of smaller data streams shaping an enormous "river" of free-text data. Information included in each such stream (and social media in general) may hamper its actual use due to shortcomings such as lack of quality control, uncertainty and trustworthiness, as well as noise and data incompleteness. However, Twitter can provide value due to the vast amount of user generated data, the user interactions and the medium's live streaming paradigm, that can be used to identify time variations on the monitoring trend.

Social media and large bibliographic libraries differ substantially. Thus, including appropriate data retrieval mechanisms for both streaming ("data rivers" like social media) and archived data sources ("data lakes" like bibliographic libraries) was conceived as a key feature of our platform.

3.2   Platform Modules

According to the micro-services architectural paradigm, each module of the proposed platform is organized as an independent web service (as explained in Sect. 3.4), typically used by an application-specific software agent. The main platform modules are (Fig. 1):

- *Data Retriever* (DR): Retrieves the data from the respective free-text data sources.
- *Text Repository* (TR): Provides the functionality of storing and querying the free-text data used by the platform's client applications.

- *Semantic Triple Store* (STS): Provides the capability of storing and retrieving data in the Resource Description Framework (RDF)[4] format, i.e. as RDF triples.
- *UIMA Annotator* (UA): Provides NLP capabilities to the respective client applications and employs the SCC module to obtain annotations in a Linked Data format.

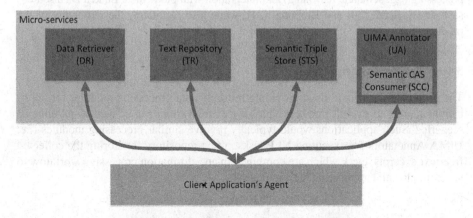

Fig. 1. The main modules of the proposed platform.

3.3   Annotation of NLP Results via Linked Data

The Linked Data paradigm is based on interlinking data using "machine-understandable" formats, in order to unambiguously define resources and concepts [2]. Adopting Linked Data as knowledge representational format facilitates the use of automatic semantic reasoning capabilities based on reusable knowledge structures, i.e. ontologies [28]. The advantages of using Linked Data in domains such as pharmacology [29] or other domains of medical interest such as epidemiology [24] can be:

- *Interoperability:* Linked Data standards e.g. RDF are based on Uniform Resource Identifiers (URIs), in order to unambiguously identify resources and concepts to facilitate communication.
- *Formal semantics:* Linked Data standards such as RDF and Web Ontology Language (OWL) define formal semantic relations between resources (e.g. classes, subclasses, cardinality restrictions, etc.) based on robust logic (e.g. OWL semantics are based on Description Logics).
- *Automatic inferencing:* Formal semantic relations can be used for automatic inferencing and reasoning via off-the-shelf software reasoners (e.g. Hermit[5]).
- *Knowledge reuse:* The interconnection of various publicly available data sources via Linked Data standards can facilitate their reuse and possible extension.

The platform's NLP results are formatted as RDF graphs by the SCC module and then typically stored via the STS web service. The SCC output RDF graphs are based on W3C's

---

[4] https://www.w3.org/RDF/.

[5] http://www.hermit-reasoner.com/.

Web Annotation Data Model (WADM)[6] and SNOMED-CT[7]. WADM is a W3C recommendation used to annotate resources (web pages, videos, free-text excerpts, etc.) in an interoperable and machine-understandable fashion. SNOMED-CT is a widely-used thesaurus of clinical terms. Using RDF, WADM and SNOMED-CT facilitates further processing (e.g. semantic reasoning) and integration with biomedical Linked Data sources such as Bio2RDF [30] and BioPortal [31], while also facilitating the reusability of the produced outcomes.

3.4   Micro-services Approach

The proposed platform aims at providing reusable data processing modules for applications aiming to exploit free-text data sources for various public health surveillance scenarios. Such applications would typically involve similar processing modules (i.e. UIMA Annotators for executing NLP tasks, a text repository for storing the collected free-text excerpts, etc.), which are combined in an information processing workflow to accommodate the application requirements.

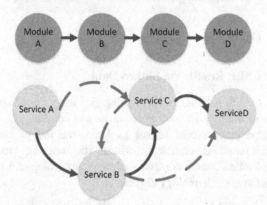

Fig. 2. Comparison of workflow paradigms, implied by the platform modules' deployment approach. On the upper part, the fixed modules' setup enforces a static pipeline workflow ("linked list" paradigm). On the lower part, modules deployed as micro-services can be used in variant application workflows ("graph" paradigm). The graph edges' line pattern (solid or dashed line) implies alternative workflows, i.e. using services in the context of different applications as part of different workflows.

However, the workflows of data processing and use of such modules are application-specific and, thus, could radically change among applications. In order to maximize the impact of the development effort and increase the provided modules reusability, the platform design does not commit in a "hard coded" workflow. Instead of hardwiring the developed modules in a pipeline similar to a linked list representing a typical application

---

[6] http://www.w3.org/TR/annotation-model/.
[7] http://www.ihtsdo.org/snomed-ct.

workflow, we envisaged our software modules as nodes of a services' graph and deployed them using a micro-services oriented approach. Each application uses the provided services combined in an application-specific processing pipeline, which forms a path among the respective graph nodes, as shown in Fig. 2.

Micro-services is an architectural paradigm which is based on providing the target data-processing functionality through simple independent web services [3, 32] (usually RESTful [33]), providing benefits regarding development, maintenance and reusability of the various software modules. Among such benefits are [3]:

- *Robustness to failure*: If one of the provided services fails, the client applications can still work with the others.
- *Decentralized data management*: The management of the results produced by the services take place at the client application's side, decoupling the provided processing service from the client application specific data processing.
- *Evolutionary design*: New services are deployed without affecting or being affected by already existing ones, facilitating platform maintenance and scalability.

The main advantage of the micro-services approach in the proposed platform's context is that the various modules can be developed and maintained independently of the specific application scenario and the respective processing workflow. Therefore, the same modules (e.g. UIMA Annotator and Text Repository) can be used in a variety of similar applications, complying with the graph path-workflow paradigm (Fig. 2).

4 Results

In this section, we provide implementation details concerning the platform modules and illustrate their use in the scope of the proof-of-concept application scenario.

4.1 Platform Implementation

Data Retriever (DR). The DR module has been developed using Java[TM]. The data retrieval process is triggered through a REST Application Programming Interface (API) call. The REST API call contains the keywords to be searched and the time range of the search. The result is in general a stream and not a fixed set of free-text excerpts. Therefore, the client application's agent has two retrieval options for the results: (a) they can be returned to a specific client HTTP endpoint, or (b) they can be saved directly to the platform's TR. Typically, a client application exploiting the proposed platform's web services would use the second option, as it is easier to use. PubMed abstracts are collected through periodic calls to the Europe PMC Web services[8]. Respectively, tweets containing the requested key phrases are retrieved via the Twitter Streaming API[9].

---

[8] http://europepmc.org/RestfulWebService.
[9] https://dev.twitter.com/streaming/overview.

Text Repository (TR). The TR module has been implemented using Apache Solr[10]. Solr provides a REST API to retrieve, save, update or delete data in a secure and efficient manner, while providing a user-friendly interface to explore excerpts. It is typically used in enterprise systems to index text data and provide search functionality in a scalable fashion.

Semantic Triple Store (STS). The STS module has been deployed using OpenLink Virtuoso as the backend engine[11]. Virtuoso provides a SPARQL Graph Store HTTP Protocol[12] compatible interface, namely a REST API, which is used to save or query RDF triples. Furthermore, Virtuoso provides a suite of web interface based tools to facilitate manual data queries for exploratory reasons and other data management and maintenance operations.

UIMA Annotator (UA) and the Semantic CAS Consumer (SCC). The UA module is built upon the Apache UIMA open-source Java Software Development Kit (SDK). More specifically, the NLP modules of Apache cTAKES [34] have been used, in order to annotate the retrieved texts according to UMLS[13] thesauri via the so-called Aggregate Plain Text UMLS Annotator. These annotations are further processed by a simple, custom ADR Annotator, which annotates free-text excerpts as possible ADR signals, aligned with the scope of the proof-of-concept application. The UA is used through a simple REST API, where the client has two options to define the text excerpts to be analyzed: (a) the excerpts are sent as part of the HTTP request, or (b) a TR excerpt collection can be named and then the UA retrieves the excerpts directly from the TR. The analysis results are returned in an asynchronous fashion using one of the two available options: (a) the result set is returned to a specific client HTTP endpoint, or (b) saved directly to the platform's STS module.

Apache UIMA NLP analysis workflow is based on the so-called Aggregate Analysis Engine (AAE), which is composed of many Annotators. The analysis results are stored in the Common Analysis Structure (CAS), which is an in-memory data structure shared between the various Annotators. Finally, a CAS Consumer module handles the results after analysis is complete. Usually, a CAS Consumer gets the results from CAS and translates them in an application-specific format (e.g. saves them in a database). UIMA allows the integration of custom analysis modules (e.g. Annotators, CAS Consumers, etc.) in the analysis workflow as part of the respective AAEs.

We developed and integrated the SCC in the platform's AAE, in order to export the analysis results as RDF triples. SCC accesses the UIMA CAS after all the NLP annotators have finished analyzing raw data, iterates through the in-memory analysis results, adds the respective RDF statements to the produced output and, finally, returns the results either by storing them in STS or by sending them to the client application. The SCC has been developed using Apache Jena[14].

---

[10] http://lucene.apache.org/solr/.
[11] http://virtuoso.openlinksw.com/.
[12] https://www.w3.org/TR/sparql11-http-rdf-update/.
[13] http://www.nlm.nih.gov/research/umls/.
[14] https://jena.apache.org/.

4.2   Proof-of-Concept Application

The first proof-of-concept application utilizing the proposed platform aims at identifying candidate ADR signals from PubMed and Twitter data. Figure 3 depicts the proof-of-concept application workflow. The first step is data retrieval through the DR and then storage in the TR module. The next step involves the analysis of the collected data through NLP techniques using the UA module. The collected excerpts are annotated through the UA and SCC and the results are stored in the STS. Finally, the obtained candidate ADR signals are compared with DrugBank[15], which is used as the reference source to filter known ADRs and preserve only the novel indications as candidates for further review (causality assessment). This last step, is part of the client application specific data processing workflow and is not provided from the platform's web services.

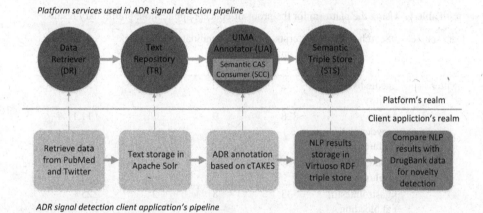

Fig. 3. Using platform modules for the proof-of-concept application (dark boxes in the bottom-right part denote processing using Semantic Web technologies).

In the scope of the ADR signal detection scenario, the entire archive of PubMed abstracts and Twitter posts collected within a 6-month period have been searched for four severe health conditions, namely, "acute liver injury", "acute myocardial infarction", "acute renal failure", and "gastrointestinal bleeding". The final aim of the application is to identify potential expressions denoting a causal relation between drugs and the above-mentioned health conditions and assess whether these are novel or not (cf. the signal definition provided in Sect. 1) using DrugBank. Twitter and PubMed have been used for ADR signal detection in other studies as well. According to [1], approximately 13,000 new ADR-related articles are indexed in PubMed each year, while Twitter may contain personal experiences of drug use shared among networked communities [14].

---

[15] http://www.drugbank.ca/.

Table 1 depicts the respective health conditions of interest and some preliminary results of the proposed platform's micro-services usage in the context of the proof-of-concept application. It should be noted that these results are based on a simple custom ADR signal annotator, which annotates a sentence as a candidate ADR signal whenever: (a) any drug and (b) the considered medical conditions are mentioned in the same sentence. The lack of identifying causal expressions linking the drug and the condition is the reason of the high percentage of unconfirmed ADR signals as it has a profound impact on the way that ADR candidate signals are recognized. However, the precision of the ADR signals annotator is considered out of the current paper's scope, which focuses on the platform rather than the proof-of-concept application. The confirmation of the candidate ADR signals against the DrugBank reference dataset is performed using the RDF version of DrugBank provided by Bio2RDF [16].

Table 1. Using the platform for the proof-of-concept application: preliminary results

Data source	Search term	Excerpts' total number	UA candidate signals	DrugBank confirmed ADRs	Confirmed signals percentage
Twitter	acute liver injury	32	0	0	N/A
	acute myocardial infarction	828	9	1	11.11%
	acute renal failure	561	11	2	18.2%
	gastrointestinal bleeding	533	8	2	25%
PubMed	acute liver injury	1,274	81	0	0%
	acute myocardial infarction	47,609	1,280	48	3.75%
	acute renal failure	43,101	1,740	48	2.75%
	gastrointestinal bleeding	11,892	400	12	3%

Figure 4 presents an example annotation that the proposed platform generated in the context of the proof-of-concept application. The example ADR is that Acetaminophen (drug) could cause acute liver injury (condition), found in a sentence contained in a specific PubMed abstract. The SCC module forms the results of the custom ADR annotator as an OWL ontology, compatible with WADM while referencing SNOMED-CT. Since SNOMED-CT does not have an official RDF serialization, the SNOMED CT URI Standard

---

[16] http://bio2rdf.org/.

[35] has been used to reference SNOMED-CT terms (namely "Drug" or "Adverse drug reaction").

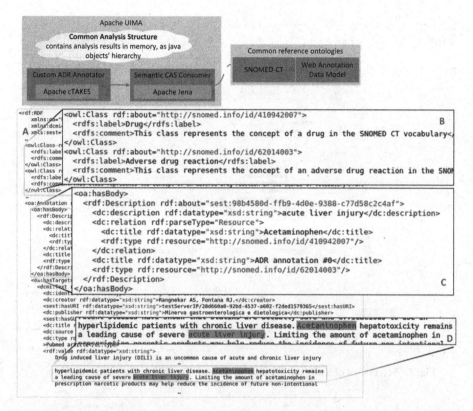

Fig. 4. Excerpt of the semantic enrichment applied on the UIMA analysis results, focusing on the use of WADM and SNOMED-CT, in order to reference concepts of "Drug" and "Adverse drug reaction" (section A: the overall OWL annotation; section B: definition of classes according to SNOMED-CT; section C: annotation body, and section D: annotation target highlighting the two relevant terms).

The example in Fig. 4 depicts an Annotation, which has a *Body* and a *Target*. The Body (Fig. 4, Sect. C) refers to the annotation itself and the Target refers to the original excerpt. The "acute liver injury" condition is an instance of the SCC output's OWL class labelled "Adverse drug reaction" and references the SNOMED-CT term with ID 62014003 (Fig. 4, Sect. B). Furthermore, Acetaminophen is an instance of the SCC output's OWL class named "Drug" referencing the SNOMED-CT ID 410942007 using the SNOMED CT URI convention (Fig. 4, Sect. B).

Figure 5 shows an example of using the TR module's web-based user interface to explore the collected results. The screenshot shows a collected tweet containing the message "To take the third and fourth *aspirin* and risk *gastrointestinal bleeding* or continue on with a headache…". A concern about a possible ADR is identified in the specific tweet (as it refers to the drug "aspirin" and the medical condition "gastrointestinal bleeding") and this ADR mention has been verified in our client application's workflow using DrugBank.

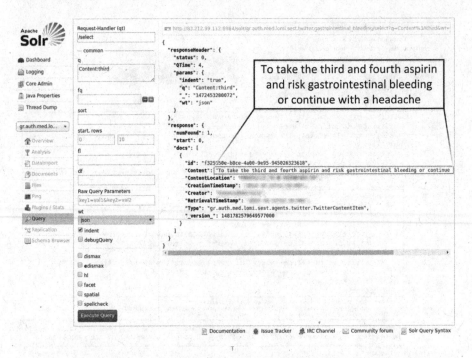

Fig. 5. Screenshot of using the TR module through the Apache Solr Web interface.

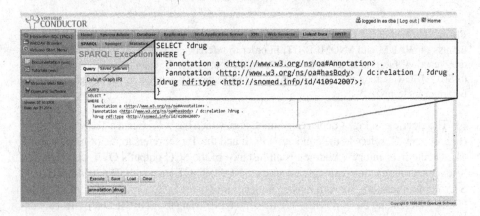

Fig. 6. Screenshot of using the Apache Solr Web interface of the TR module.

Figure 6 shows an example of using the STS module's web-based user interface to explore the produced WADM annotations. In particular, the screenshot shows the use of the Virtuoso Triple Store web-based interface in formulating a SPARQL query against the collected annotations, in order to explore the semantically annotated results stored in the STS. The example SPARQL query would return all the drugs identified by the platform's SCC in the collected free-text snippets.

5 Discussion

This paper presented the design of an IT platform aiming to support the systematic exploitation of free-text data sources for public health surveillance applications and a proof-of-concept application aiming at identifying candidate ADR signals. In this section, we summarize our contribution focusing on the two main key design principles, namely (a) using the micro-services architectural approach, and (b) using Linked Data as the main data representation format. Furthermore, we describe the lessons learned from the platform development so far, and briefly refer to future work plans.

5.1 Contribution

Typically, the systems developed to monitor data sources for public health surveillance scenarios (as referred to Sect. 2) are application-specific and, thus, too narrow in scope, hampering generalization of their underlying IT framework.

In the presented platform, the micro-services architecture paradigm has been adopted in order to decouple the application scenarios from the provided information services and allow their reusability in multiple application workflows, using an easy to use and standards-based REST communication interface. The use of REST as communication paradigm allows the platform modules' and the client applications' independent development, avoiding dependencies on specific programming languages or operating systems, while allowing the use of ready, out-of-the-box software libraries for handling low-level communication. Moreover, the micro-services architecture paradigm provides flexibility regarding adding new services in the future, in order to support new application scenarios and processing workflows, while still reusing existing platform modules. Furthermore, the suggested approach facilitates the scalability of the overall platform, as each main platform's functionality is deployed as an independent service module. In case of one module acting as a performance bottleneck, the scaling actions (e.g. computation resources assignment, configuration changes, etc.) could be more targeted and focused on the specific service module, avoiding the complexity of scaling the overall functionality.

The developed SCC is considered a major contribution of the platform, as it enables the representation of UIMA NLP analysis results using Linked Data formalisms and, therefore, facilitates interoperability and further processing. The SCC references the SNOMED-CT common terminology and uses the WADM annotation model. While a CAS Consumer converting UIMA results to RDF already exists[17], it is based on a rather heavy Open Services Gateway initiative (OSGi) framework, hindering its integration in

---

[17] https://uima.apache.org/downloads/sandbox/RDF_CC/RDFCASConsumerUserGuide.html.

other applications. Moreover, the specific OSGi-based CAS Consumer does not apply any semantic enrichment of the results, which is one of the SCC key features.

Finally, one of the presented platform's key benefits is the integration of heterogeneous data sources, i.e. streaming data sources (such as Twitter), following the "data river" paradigm, and large archived databases (such as PubMed), following the "data lake" paradigm.

Summarizing the presented platform's overall contribution, it first facilitates the systematic real-time aggregation of free-text data sources with different characteristics. The standards-based semantic integration of the collected data could significantly facilitate further processing (e.g. knowledge engineering, analytics, etc.). These characteristics are very useful in public health surveillance applications, like the ADR signal detection scenario that we elaborated as a proof-of-concept.

5.2   Limitations and Lessons Learned

The main difficulty of using a micro-services approach is keeping each service's functionality generic and independent of the client application. While offering generic data storage services has been addressed successfully, generalizing the analysis services is far from trivial, since these are typically coupled with the respective analysis scenario. In particular, keeping the UA module independent of the specific ADR signal proof-of-concept application, while still providing added value for the specific application, has proven to be a major challenge. The UA module exploits annotators engaged in its specific UIMA workflow. Therefore, the UA module can be reused in other applications targeting ADRs, since it includes such an annotator. However, generalizing its use in other application scenarios, not related with ADRs, would require further development or change on its UIMA workflow.

Using Linked Data as the main data representation format introduces additional challenges. For example, while SNOMED-CT is a widely-accepted resource, there is no official RDF representation and an "unofficial" conversion scheme is used. The same problem applies for many other, widely accepted thesauri and this could hinder their integration in future applications. Moreover, while platforms like Bio2RDF translate widely used data sources to RDF, these translation mechanisms can be complex, introduce errors or time lag and, therefore, the RDF versions are not updated, credible or easy to use and verify as the original ones.

5.3   Future Work

We currently explore text storage using NoSQL technologies to address requirements regarding performance and scalability. Particularly, we elaborate on integrating MongoDB[18] as the TR's backend, in order to facilitate scaling and maintenance activities.

Moreover, further meta-analysis capabilities are investigated through the exploitation of semantic reasoning techniques. In the proposed platform's context, a plethora of public biomedical ontologies could be used to advance further data processing (e.g.

---

[18] https://www.mongodb.com/.

ontologies in BioPortal or Bio2RDF datasets). Further integration with Linked Data sources like the ones provided by Bio2RDF and the development of a reasoning module service are planned. This module would provide generic semantic reasoning capabilities to be used by the client applications.

Additionally, we currently work on facilitating changes in the UA analysis workflow, in order to allow client applications to select the UIMA annotators engaged in the requested analysis workflow. We also explore ways of further generalizing the mapping between UIMA analysis results and standard terminologies. In particular, the automatic matching of the UMLS annotations generated by Apache cTAKES with UMLS URIs is being investigated, in order to allow the UA and SCC modules to be even more application-independent.

For the ADR proof-of-concept application per se, the annotation results are currently analyzed, while the final goal is to perform integrated signal detection through the concurrent exploitation of both sources [22, 36]. Furthermore, ways to improve the custom ADR annotator are investigated.

As an ultimate goal, we plan to release the platform in an open-source repository along with the detailed documentation of its APIs and example scenarios. The public deployment of our platform requires a lot of work regarding performance, resource management, security, etc. We currently work on cloud infrastructure issues to facilitate the platform's public use.

References

1. Harpaz, R., Callahan, A., Tamang, S., Low, Y., Odgers, D., Finlayson, S., Jung, K., LePendu, P., Shah, N.H.: Text mining for adverse drug events: the promise, challenges, and state of the art. Drug Saf. **37**, 777–790 (2014)
2. Bizer, C.: The emerging web of Linked Data. IEEE Intell. Syst. **24**, 87–92 (2009)
3. Martin Fowler: Microservices. http://martinfowler.com/articles/microservices.html
4. Apache UIMA - Apache UIMA. http://uima.apache.org/
5. Sarker, A., Ginn, R., Nikfarjam, A., O'Connor, K., Smith, K., Jayaraman, S., Upadhaya, T., Gonzalez, G.: Utilizing social media data for pharmacovigilance: a review. J. Biomed. Inform. **54**, 202–212 (2015)
6. Council for International Organizations of Medical Sciences (CIOMS): Practical Aspects of Signal Detection in Pharmacovigilance. Council for International Organizations of Medical Sciences. Report of CIOMS Working Group VIII. CIOMS, Geneva (2010)
7. Klann, J.G., Buck, M.D., Brown, J., Hadley, M., Elmore, R., Weber, G.M., Murphy, S.N.: Query Health: standards-based, cross-platform population health surveillance. J. Am. Med. Inform. Assoc. **21**, 650–656 (2014)
8. Teodoro, D., Pasche, E., Gobeill, J., Emonet, S., Ruch, P., Lovis, C.: Building a transnational biosurveillance network using Semantic Web technologies: requirements, design, and preliminary evaluation. J. Med. Internet Res. **14**(3), e73 (2012)
9. Daniulaityte, R., Chen, L., Lamy, F.R., Carlson, R.G., Thirunarayan, K., Sheth, A.: When "Bad" is "Good": identifying personal communication and sentiment in drug-related tweets. JMIR Public Heal. Surveill. **2**, e162 (2016)
10. Huff, A.G., Breit, N., Allen, T., Whiting, K., Kiley, C.: Evaluation and verification of the global rapid identification of threats system for infectious diseases in textual data sources. Interdiscip. Perspect. Infect. Dis. **2016**, 5080746 (2016)

11. Yang, M., Kiang, M., Shang, W.: Filtering big data from social media – building an early warning system for adverse drug reactions. J. Biomed. Inform. **54**, 230–240 (2015)
12. Cameron, D., Smith, G.A., Daniulaityte, R., Sheth, A.P., Dave, D., Chen, L., Anand, G., Carlson, R., Watkins, K.Z., Falck, R.: PREDOSE: a Semantic Web platform for drug abuse epidemiology using social media. J. Biomed. Inform. **46**, 985–997 (2013)
13. Shang, N., Xu, H., Rindflesch, T.C., Cohen, T.: Identifying plausible adverse drug reactions using knowledge extracted from the literature. J. Biomed. Inform. **52**, 293–310 (2014)
14. Freifeld, C.C., Brownstein, J.S., Menone, C.M., Bao, W., Filice, R., Kass-Hout, T., Dasgupta, N.: Digital drug safety surveillance: monitoring pharmaceutical products in Twitter. Drug Saf. **37**, 343–350 (2014)
15. Chew, C., Eysenbach, G.: Pandemics in the age of Twitter: content analysis of tweets during the 2009 H1N1 outbreak. PLoS ONE **5**, e14118 (2010)
16. Ram, S., Zhang, W., Williams, M., Pengetnze, Y.: Predicting asthma-related emergency department visits using big data. IEEE J. Biomed. Heal. Inform. **19**, 1216–1223 (2015)
17. Gesualdo, F., Stilo, G., D'Ambrosio, A., Carloni, E., Pandolfi, E., Velardi, P., Fiocchi, A., Tozzi, A.E.: Can Twitter be a source of information on allergy? correlation of pollen counts with tweets reporting symptoms of allergic rhinoconjunctivitis and names of antihistamine drugs. PLoS ONE **10**, e0133706 (2015)
18. Gittelman, S., Lange, V., Gotway Crawford, C.A., Okoro, C.A., Lieb, E., Dhingra, S.S., Trimarchi, E.: A new source of data for public health surveillance: Facebook likes. J. Med. Internet Res. **17**(4), e98 (2015)
19. Fullwood, M.D., Kecojevic, A., Basch, C.H.: Examination of YouTube videos related to synthetic cannabinoids. Int. J. Adolesc. Med. Health (2016)
20. Shin, S.-Y., Seo, D.-W., An, J., Kwak, H., Kim, S.-H., Gwack, J., Jo, M.-W.: High correlation of Middle East respiratory syndrome spread with google search and Twitter trends in Korea. Sci. Rep. **6**, 32920 (2016)
21. Santillana, M., Nguyen, A.T., Dredze, M., Paul, M.J., Nsoesie, E.O., Brownstein, J.S.: Combining search, social media, and traditional data sources to improve influenza surveillance. PLoS Comput. Biol. **11**, e1004513 (2015)
22. Koutkias, V., Lillo-Le Louët, A., Jaulent, M.C.: Exploiting heterogeneous publicly available data sources for drug safety surveillance: computational framework and case studies. Expert Opin. Drug Saf. **16**, 113–124 (2016)
23. Poulymenopoulou, M., Papakonstantinou, D., Malamateniou, F., Vassilacopoulos, G.: A health analytics semantic ETL service for obesity surveillance. Stud. Health Technol. Inform. **210**, 840–844 (2015)
24. Chorianopoulos, K., Talvis, K.: Flutrack.org: open-source and Linked Data for epidemiology. Health Inform. J. **22**(4), 962–974 (2015)
25. Kato, Y., Izui, T., Murakawa, Y., Okabayashi, K., Ueki, M., Tsuchiya, Y., Narita, M.: Research and development environments for robot services and its implementation. In: 2011 IEEE/SICE International Symposium on System Integration (SII), pp. 306–311 (2011)
26. Vögler, M., Schleicher, J., Inzinger, C., Nastic, S., Sehic, S., Dustdar, S.: LEONORE – large-scale provisioning of resource-constrained IoT deployments. In: 9th International Symposium on Service-Oriented System Engineering, pp. 78–87 (2015)
27. Ono, K., Muetze, T., Kolishovski, G., Shannon, P., Demchak, B.: CyREST: turbocharging cytoscape access for external tools via a RESTful API. F1000Research **4**, 478 (2015)
28. Fages, F., Soliman, S. (eds.): PPSWR 2005. LNCS, vol. 3703. Springer, Heidelberg (2005)
29. Samwald, M., Jentzsch, A., Bouton, C., Kallesøe, C.S., Willighagen, E., Hajagos, J., Marshall, M.S., Prud'hommeaux, E., Hassenzadeh, O., Pichler, E., Stephens, S.: Linked open drug data for pharmaceutical research and development. J Cheminform. **3**, 19 (2011)

30. Callahan, A., Cruz-Toledo, J., Ansell, P., Dumontier, M.: Bio2RDF release 2: improved coverage, interoperability and provenance of life science Linked Data. In: Cimiano, P., Corcho, O., Presutti, V., Hollink, L., Rudolph, S. (eds.) The Semantic Web: Semantics and Big Data, pp. 200–212. Springer, Heidelberg (2013)

31. Salvadores, M., Alexander, P.R., Musen, M.A., Noy, N.F.: BioPortal as a dataset of linked biomedical ontologies and terminologies in RDF. Semant. Web. **4**, 277–284 (2013)

32. Sneps-Sneppe, M., Namiot, D.: Micro-service architecture for emerging telecom applications. Int. J. Open Inf. Technol. **2**, 34–38 (2014)

33. Fielding, R.T., Taylor, R.N.: Principled design of the modern web architecture. In: Proceedings of the 22nd International Conference on Software Engineering, pp. 407–416. ACM, New York (2000)

34. Savova, G.K., Masanz, J.J., Ogren, P.V., Zheng, J., Sohn, S., Kipper-Schuler, K.C., Chute, C.G.: Mayo clinical text analysis and knowledge extraction system (cTAKES): architecture, component evaluation and applications. J. Am. Med. Inform. Assoc. **17**, 507–513 (2010)

35. Lawley, M.: SNOMED CT URI Standard. http://ihtsdo.org/fileadmin/user_upload/doc/download/doc_UriStandard_Current-en-US_INT_20140527.pdf?ok

36. Koutkias, V.G., Jaulent, M.-C.: Computational approaches for pharmacovigilance signal detection: toward integrated and semantically-enriched frameworks. Drug Saf. **38**, 219–232 (2015)

Computer Guideline Engineering and Usage

Knowledge-Driven Paper Retrieval
to Support Updating of Clinical Guidelines
A Use Case on PubMed

Veruska Zamborlini[1,2(✉)], Qing Hu[1], Zhisheng Huang[1], Marcos da Silveira[2],
Cedric Pruski[2], Annette ten Teije[1], and Frank van Harmelen[1]

[1] Vrije Universiteit Amsterdam, Amsterdam, The Netherlands
{v.carrettazamborlini,qhu400}@vu.nl,
{huang,annette,frank.van.harmelen}@cs.vu.nl
[2] Luxembourg Institute of Science and Technology - LIST,
Esch-sur-Alzette, Luxembourg
{marcos.dasilveira,cedric.pruski}@list.lu

Abstract. Clinical Guidelines are important knowledge resources for medical decision making. They provide clinical recommendations based on a collection of research findings with respect to a specific disease. Since, new findings are regularly published, CGs are also expected to be regularly updated. However, selecting and analysing medical publications require a huge human efforts, even when these publications are mostly regrouped and into repositories (e.g., MEDLINE database) and accessible via a search engine (e.g. PubMed). Automatically detecting those research findings from a medical search engine such as PubMed supports the guideline updating process. A simple search method is to select the medical terms that appear in the conclusions of the guideline to generate a query to search for new evidences. However, some challenges rise in this method: how to select the important terms, besides how to consider background knowledge that may be missing or not explicitly stated in those conclusions. In this paper we apply a *knowledge model* that formally describes elements such as actions and their effects to investigate (i) if it favors selecting the medical terms to compose queries and (ii) if a search enhanced with background knowledge can provide better result than other methods. This work explores a knowledge-driven approach for detecting new evidences relevant for the clinical guideline update process. Based on the outcomes of two experiments, we found that this approach can improve the recall by retrieving more relevant evidences than previous methods.

V. Zamborlini—Funded by CNPq (Brazilian National Council for Scientific and Technological Development) within the program Science without Borders.

Q. Hu—Funded by China Scholarship Council.

Z. Huang—Partially supported by Dutch National Project COMMIT/-Data2Semantics.

D. Riaño et al. (Eds.): KR4HC/ProHealth 2016, LNAI 10096, pp. 71–89, 2017.
DOI: 10.1007/978-3-319-55014-5_5

1   Introduction

Clinical guidelines (CGs) are a collection of best practices, selected based on the latest research findings. Thus, they are expected to be updated regularly and frequently to accommodate new research findings (also known as "evidences") in medicine. However, the quantity of new medical findings published almost every day increases the workload and the complexity of CGs updating tasks. For instance, almost 20.000 new papers (or almost 55 new papers per day) about *breast cancer* were added to PubMed in 2015. Reviewing all these papers to extract relevant information for CGs updating becomes a laborious work. Therefore, automatically detecting relevant papers (i.e. supported with a computer tool) and highlighting the new findings, e.g. taking as reference the PubMed dataset, is considered a relevant approach for supporting the guideline updating process.

In order to find new evidences, the experts need to define queries to be posed against a dataset, e.g. PubMed. Selecting appropriate keywords (e.g., terms from Mesh vocabulary) for building PubMed queries has been done for long time by hand. Previous work [1] had shown that PubMed queries can be constructed based on the conclusion text to find relevant papers. Guideline conclusions are the summaries of a number of medical evidences on which the guideline recommendations are based (e.g. *After a radiation boost the risk of local recurrence of breast cancer is lower*). However, simply considering all medical terms from the conclusions may decrease the performance of the tools (their disjunction generates a huge quantity of papers to review, or their conjunction may exclude relevant papers from the results). In [2,3], we propose an approach for detecting new and relevant evidences for clinical guideline update, by using a semantic-distance measure for ranking the medical terms extracted from guideline conclusions. The ranked terms are selected to generate PubMed queries used to find the evidences. That semantics-distance-based approach can provide a better result for the search, compared with previous approach [1]. However, we found that some guideline conclusions are weakly linked to their targeted evidences, i.e. the terms used in the conclusions are not enough to retrieve all the relevant evidences. How to obtain the medical terms in order to optimise the performance of the search system remains an open issue.

The goal of this work is on the one hand to investigate if a knowledge-driven approach can favor addressing the aforementioned open issue and, on the other hand, to investigate the applicability of the TMR (Transition-based medical Recommendation) model for supporting the guideline update task. This model is meant for representing knowledge underlying clinical guidelines, and has been applied to address the multimorbidity issue [4]. Therefore, we propose a method for automatically constructing PubMed queries from formal representation of the CGs conclusions based on the TMR model. The method relies on its causation structure, namely actions and effects, for both selecting medical terms and guiding 4 possible logical patterns for building the queries. It allows for enriching the original terms provided in the conclusions with alternative descriptions.

We have conducted two experiments on the Dutch Clinical Guidelines of Breast Cancer. We formalize some conclusions from the older version, submit the automatically generated queries to PubMed and verify if we find at least the list of publications referenced by the corresponding conclusion in the new version of the CG. This list of publications references is named in this paper as *goal evidences*. We analyse the results and compare to the results obtained in our previous approach.

This paper is organized as follows. The fully automatic approach previously mentioned, the semantic-distance method, is presented in Sect. 2. Sections 3 and 4 describe the TMR model applied for guideline update and the method for automatic query construction based on this model. Section 5 reports the experiments and results. Discussion and conclusion are presented in Sects. 6 and 7.

2   Semantic-Distance Method for Guideline Update

Evidence-based clinical guidelines rely on published scientific research findings. Those publications are usually available in Web-based biomedical databases, like PubMed. In [2,3], we proposed a semantic distance method for automatic detecting new evidences for guideline update. The main challenge consists in how to select relevant medical terms to compose a query for retrieving new medical evidences from datasets such as PubMed. Indeed, simply using all the terms as conjunction or disjunction has been shown not to be effective. The semantic distance measure is based on the (widely shared) assumption that the more frequently co-occurring terms exist the more semantically related they are. Based on this measure the terms are ranked and selected via an heuristic function developed based on three criteria: term coverage, evidence coverage and bounding number. We have reported several experiments to evaluate this approach. We selected the Dutch breast cancer guideline (version 1.0, 2004) [5] and the Dutch breast cancer guideline (version 2.0, 2012) [6] as the test data.

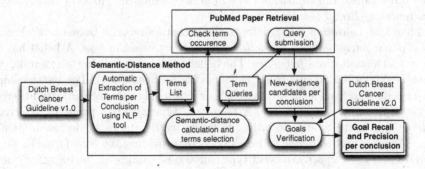

Fig. 1. Experiments' workflow for applying semantic distance approach for the Dutch Breast Cancer guidelines.

Figure 1 depicts a workflow of the general idea applied in the aforementioned experiments. Firstly, the original guideline [5] is the input for automatic extraction of a list of relevant medical terms. To do so a NLP tool is applied to the text of each guideline conclusion and the heading of the sections or subsections, producing a list of medical terms according to UMLS vocabulary. Then, the semantic distance is calculated for each term by checking its occurrence in PubMed articles. The terms are ranked and the most important ones are selected to compose the term-queries to be submitted to PubMed. From the retrieved publications, it is verified if the expected goals per conclusion are achieved (based on [6]), and the respective recall and precision are calculated.

From these experiments, we concluded that improvements are still needed in order to reduce the size of the obtained results and to find more goal evidence for more guideline items. We observed that some guideline conclusions are weakly linked to their targeted evidences, i.e. in some cases the exact terms used in the conclusions are not enough to retrieve all the relevant evidences.

3   TMR Model Applied for Guideline Update

The TMR model has been developed for representing knowledge underlying CGs, aiming at supporting different guideline-related tasks. In our previous work [4,7] we addressed the task of combining several guidelines (multimorbidity) by automatically detecting interactions among recommendations. In this paper we will: (i) check the applicability of the TMR model on supporting the update task and (ii) identify improvements required to better address this task.

Figure 2 presents an excerpt of the UML class diagram of the TMR model, including at the bottom an example of instantiation. The model addresses the guideline as source of medical conclusions, which are beliefs about a causation relation[1]. In the example, *"After a **boost** the **risk of local recurrence** is lower"* is a conclusion/belief (*CB#1*) from the Dutch Breast Cancer Guideline about the causation relation between two event types: the action *boost (of radiation dose)* often causes the transition (*Tr#1*) of decreasing the property *risk of local recurrence (of Breast Cancer)*[2].

Therefore, *causation beliefs* refer to the causation relation between two *event types*; particularly between an *action type* and a *transition type*. A belief has a *source* and a (causation) *frequency*. The belief can be simple as in the example, or it can be composed, having other beliefs as its *part* (*hasPart*). The relationship *causes* is derived from a causation belief (or exists only in its context) and therefore is depicted as a dotted line. A transition type *affects* a property, referred as *trope type* in the model, according to its *derivative* (increase, decrease, maintain). Another way to define a transition is by providing the *transformable* and *expected Situation Types*. An event type can also be composed, having other ones as its *part* (*hasPart*). All the elements can have *description*(s). In particular, the

---

[1] The relation to the evidences will be addressed in future work.

[2] This is our interpretation, as the conclusion itself is not very precise.

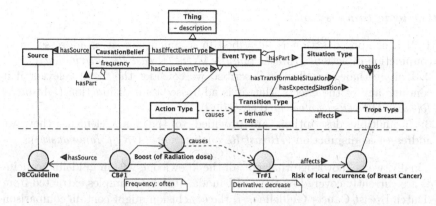

Fig. 2. UML class diagram for an excerpt of the TMR model.

composition of either beliefs or event types are added in this work, as it was not required in previous work for applying the TMR model[3].

We advocate that this excerpt of the TMR model contains essential information for searching for new evidences, namely **action and effect** (sometimes the expected situation has a description, like *fever*, sometimes it is the property affected by the transition, like *temperature*). It allows to offer four options for how to query for papers by varying the logic composition of actions and effects, which we call query patterns. The first two patterns are simple consultation for publications regarding either actions or effects, and the last two are conjunction and disjunction combinations of the previous ones.

Query Patterns

QP1 - Action: this pattern allows for retrieving any publication referring to the action in a conclusion. For example, to retrieve papers about new/unknown effects for that action (e.g. *Silicon Implant*);

QP2 - Effect: this pattern allows for retrieving any publication referring to the effect in a conclusion. For example, to retrieve papers about new/unknown actions that produce or interfere in that effect (e.g. *Systemic Syndrome*);

QP3 - Action AND Effect: this is a more strict pattern that allows for retrieving publications referring simultaneously to both action and effect (e.g. *(Silicon Implant)+AND+(Systemic Syndrome)*);

QP4 - Action OR Effect: this pattern accumulates the results of 1 and 2 (e.g. *(Silicon Implant)+OR+(Systemic Syndrome)*).

Moreover, the conclusions might refer to more than one action or effect, as well as multiple descriptions for the same element can be found in the guideline itself or in external vocabularies. In the sequel we present and justify other logic compositions for each of these cases:

---

[3] For sake of readability, hereafter we omit mentioning "type" for the model elements.

Other logic compositions

LC1: If a composed action is described in a conclusion, it is addressed as a conjunction of actions (*(Mastectomy)+AND+(Breast Reconstruction)*);

LC2: If more than one effect is described we consider the result relevant if it contains any of the effects, thus it is addressed as a disjunction (*(Aesthetic Result)+OR+(Psychological Well-being)*).

LC3: If multiple descriptions are provided to the same element, they are addressed as disjunction (*(Breast Reconstruction)+OR+(Mamaplasty)*);

Finally, we acknowledge that not all the knowledge within guideline conclusions are currently covered by the TMR model. Taking examples extracted from the Dutch Breast Cancer Guideline, (i) the conclusion might contain comparison of the outcome of a certain intervention with other ones or with no intervention (e.g. in Table 1 conclusion 5_1); or (ii) it might describe risk factors (e.g. "*young age (≤40 years) is an independent (negative) risk factor for the development of local recurrence after BCT (Breast-Conserving Therapy).*"). Those topics and their role on searching new evidences will be addressed in future work.

4   Extracting PubMed-Queries from TMR Model

We propose a method for investigating the applicability of the TMR model and in sequence we discuss the implementation and the design choices required to this end. Finally, SPARQL queries are provided for automatically extracting the descriptions that are relevant for constructing a search query[4]. For the experiment we chose to apply query-pattern QP3 (action AND effect) to have the results comparable to [2, 3].

4.1   Experiment Method

In the previous approach [2,3] the main challenge was to select and combine from the guideline conclusions the important terms to construct the PubMed queries (see Sect. 2). In order to understand the improvements that can be achieved by using the TMR model, we propose an experiment in two parts:

TMR-Strategy 1 - Without intervention on conclusion content: only the original description text is used for querying. It relies on synonyms provided by PubMed according to Mesh terminology.

TMR-Strategy 2 - With human intervention on conclusion content: new (alternative) descriptions are added. It assumes that: (i) relevant information is often made implicit in the conclusion; (ii) Mesh-based strategy embedded in PubMed query service provides limited options of synonyms; (iii) sometimes other related terms rather than synonyms are important (e.g. more general or more specific terms). The acquisition of such descriptions is further discussed in this paper.

---

[4] Codes are available at https://github.com/veruskacz/KR4HC2016.

Firstly, by applying TMR-STRATEGY 1 (or simply TMR-1), we investigate how the TMR knowledge-structure, particularly actions and effects, contributes for selecting important terms from a guideline conclusion. Then, given the obtained results, we analyse the missing goals and understand the reasons why they cannot be retrieved. Finally, by applying the TMR-STRATEGY 2 (or simply TMR-2), we investigate if/how the TMR model allows for the enrichment required in order to retrieve the missing goals. Observe that our claim for strategy 2 is *NOT* that now we can retrieve *ALL* the goals, since by knowing the goals we can fine tune the queries until we get what we want. The claim is that a knowledge-driven approach such as the one proposed here provides means to perform the enrichment required to improve the results in this but also in other experiments.

Figure 3 depicts at the top the workflow for applying the TMR-Strategy 1 to the Dutch Breast Cancer Guideline, and at the bottom the workflow for TMR-Strategy 2 (the experiment is reported in Sect. 5). In the former, the gray-shaded components are the same as in the Semantic Distance workflow (Fig. 1). In other words, the main change with respect to the first strategy regards the way the original guideline is processed into term-queries. The original guideline (version 1.0) is the input for the manual process of modeling the guideline conclusions according to the TMR model. The resultant structured guideline is then the input for the automatic construction of the term-queries by applying the SPARQL queries. The final output is a list of goals' recall and precision per conclusion, together with the missing goals per conclusion. The latter will

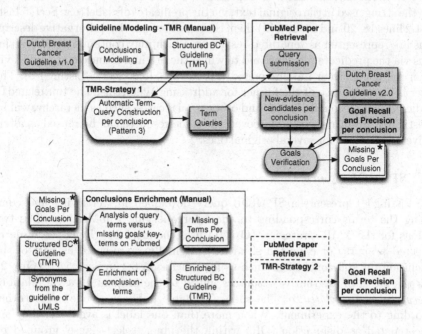

Fig. 3. Experiments' workflows for applying TRM-strategies 1 and 2.

be input for the next strategy, as well as the structured guideline, both marked with a star (*).

At the bottom part of Fig. 3, the missing goals are the input for the manual process of analyzing the terms that were missing per conclusion in order to retrieve the missing goals, according to the MESH terms used to annotate them in PubMed or the papers' titles. For the experiment, we also manually consulted UMLS vocabulary for standard descriptions as alternative for the original terms, although not everything could be (trivially) found. Moreover, the guideline itself provides alternative descriptions for a same element in several conclusions. Finally, the missing terms, together with the structured guideline and a list of synonyms (from UMLS and the guideline), is input for the process of enriching the descriptions of the conclusions terms. The enriched structured guideline is then input for applying the TMR-Strategy 2. Details are omitted for both 'dotted boxes' PubMed Paper Retrieval and TMR-Strategy 2, since they repeat the corresponding boxes in the top part. In other words, the main change in the workflow for the second experiment is the process of enriching the input for the TMR-Strategy. The final output is a new list of goals' recall and precision per conclusion.

4.2   Implementation and Design Choices

The TMR model is implemented using semantic web technologies (for more details see [4]). In order to allow for distinguishing original and alternative descriptions of guideline conclusions, some design choices are made: (i) the elements originally extracted from the conclusions are represented as RDF resources having as description the string used in the original text, via the predicate rdfs:label (e.g. Sect. 5 Listing 1.2 lines 18–20 and 26–28); (ii) then, the human-supervised alternative descriptions are represented as separated resources, which may contain several descriptions via the predicate rdfs:label and to which the original resources are linked via either tmr:relatedTo or tmr:interpretedAs predicates (e.g. Sect. 5 Listing 1.3). The latter is a special case of the former for addressing synonyms. The tmr:relatedTo predicate is intentionally broad, and other special cases, such as hierarchy, will be investigated in future work. Moreover, the same resource can be reused as alternative descriptions for several original ones.

4.3   SPARQL Queries

The Listing 1.1 presents a SPARQL query developed for retrieving and composing the terms corresponding to effect for querying PubMed. It offers two options for the TMR-strategies: **(Opt 1)** uses the *label* describing the *resource* (affected property or expected situation) originally represented as part of the conclusion (or sub-conclusions such as for conclusion 6_1 in Sect. 5.1); **(Opt 2)** uses the *labels* of alternative *resources* linked to the original ones via relations *interpretedAs* or *relatedTo*. The codes, available online, use one or the other according to the experiment. When more than one label is available, they are concatenated as disjunction (OR) within the inner 'select-clause' grouped by transition (effect), corresponding to the logic composition LC3, i.e. more than one description per element is composed as disjunction (the same holds for the code that composes the actions). The labels also need to be enclosed between parenthesis to ensure the associative properties (e.g. '(local tumor) OR (survival benefit)'). Finally the outer 'select-clause' concatenates the results of the inner 'select-clause', in this case as a disjunction (OR) grouped by conclusion ID, i.e. if more than one effect is described within an identified conclusion they are combined as disjunction according to the logic composition LC2 (for actions they would be composed as conjunction according to LC1). More examples are in Sect. 5.1. The SPARQL query for actions, available online, is slightly more complex to handle the of composition of actions.

```
   SELECT ?id (GROUP_CONCAT (?transitionLabel; separator="+OR+") AS ?term)
 2 WHERE {
   ?conclusion        rdf:type              tmr:CausationBelief .
 4 ?conclusion        tmr:conclusionID      ?id
   { GRAPH ?conclusion {      #effect is referred by the main conclusion
 6 []                 tmr:causes            ?transition }
   } UNION { ?conclusion     tmr:hasPart     ?subConclusion.
 8 GRAPH ?subConclusion {      #effect is referred by the sub-conclusion
   []                 tmr:causes            ?transition } .
10 { SELECT ?transition (CONCAT("(",GROUP_CONCAT (CONCAT("(",?label,")");
   separator="+OR+"), ")") AS ?transitionLabel)
12 WHERE {
   {?transition tmr:affects ?resource}
14 UNION {?transition tmr:hasExpectedSituation ?resource}.
   Opt1  ?resource rdfs:label  ?label.
16 Opt2  {?resource tmr:interpretedAs ?altResource}
   Opt2    UNION {?resource tmr:relatedTo ?altResource}.
18 Opt2  ?altResource rdfs:label ?label
   } GROUP BY ?transition }
20 } GROUP BY ?id
```

Listing 1.1. SPARQL code for selecting the original text (Option 1) or alternative text (Option 2) for **effects** within each conclusion, grouped by the conclusion identifier.

5 Experiments

This section reports on the experiments performed to evaluate the use of TMR model on supporting the guideline update task. We perform the retrieval of medical papers from PubMed that are relevant for updating (part of) the Dutch Breast Cancer Guideline of 2004 [5]. We evaluate the results according to a set of goal evidences used in the updated version of that guideline in 2012 [6].

5.1 Breast Cancer Guideline

Table 1 presents a set of conclusions extracted from the Dutch Breast Cancer guideline of 2004. The original conclusions are manually encoded in RDF according to the TMR model[5], with the following restrictions (see Sect. 3): (i) from the 16 conclusions updated in the new version of the guideline, 11 conclusions were selected that convey actions and their effects (rather than risk factor); and (ii) only the parts of the text regarding the main causation structure are represented.

---

[5] RDF Data is available at https://github.com/veruskacz/KR4HC2016.

Table 1. Set of conclusions from the Dutch Breast Cancer guideline of 2004, with highlighted terms corresponding to actions and effect.

ID	Conclusion text	Action	Effect
1_1	Addition of **radiotherapy** following **local excision of DCIS** results in a significantly lower **risk of local recurrence** (this is valid for all subgroups)	Radiotherapy **AND** local excision of DCIS	Risk of local recurrence
1_3	Adjuvant **therapy with tamoxifen** in **breast-conserving treatment of DCIS**, results in limited improvement of **local tumour** control and no **survival benefit**	Therapy with tamoxifen **AND** breast-conserving treatment of DCIS	Local tumour **OR** survival benefit
3_1	**Breast-conserving therapy** including **irradiation** is safe because the **survival rate** is comparable to that seen after modified radical mastectomy	Breast-conserving therapy **AND** irradiation	Survival rate
3_2	An excellent **cosmetic result** can be achieved in at least 70% of patients after **breast-conserving therapy**	Breast-conserving therapy	Cosmetic result
3_3	After a **boost** the **risk of local recurrence** is lower	Boost	Risk of local recurrence
4_1	**Postoperative locoregional radiotherapy** reduces the **risk of locoregional recurrence** by two-thirds, and results in a better **chance of survival**	Postoperative locoregional radiotherapy	Risk of locoregional recurrence **OR** chance of survival
5_1	A descriptive study found that women who undergo **breast reconstruction** immediately following the **mastectomy** are more satisfied with the **aesthetic result** and experience greater **psychosocial wellbeing**	Breast reconstruction **AND** mastectomy	Aesthetic result **OR** psychosocial wellbeing
6_1.1	There are no signs that either **primary** or **secondary breast reconstruction** results in a higher **risk of recurrent breast cancer**.	Primary breast reconstruction	Risk of recurrent breast cancer
6_1.2		Secondary breast reconstruction	risk of recurrent breast cancer
6_2	There are no indications to suggest that a **skin-sparing mastectomy** followed by **immediate reconstruction** leads to a higher **risk of local** or **systemic recurrence of breast cancer**.	Skin-sparing mastectomy **AND** immediate reconstruction	Risk of local recurrence of breast cancer **OR** risk of systemic recurrence of breast cancer
7_1	There is no causal relationship between **silicone implants** and the occurrence of **systemic syndromes**	Silicone implants	Systemic syndromes
8_1	**Radiotherapy** is associated with significantly more **complications** in the presence of a **breast reconstruction**	Radiotherapy **AND** breast reconstruction	Complications

Other parts, as previously mentioned, will be addressed in future work. Another observation is that conclusion 6_1 is divided into two conclusions according to the TMR model, to which we refer as 6_1.1 and 6_1.2. This is because the two actions mentioned in the text are not a composed action that causes the referred effect, but as two alternative actions causing the same effect. Moreover, even when effects (or affected properties) are mentioned as conjunction, such as in conclusion 1_3 (*local tumor control AND no survival benefit*), saying that both effects are expected, we are interested to retrieve papers that says something about any of them. Actually, these conclusions can be the summary of two (or more) different papers talking about one or another effect. Therefore we combine them as disjunction (OR) according to LC2.

The Listing 1.2 presents the RDF representation of (part of) the conclusion 5_1 according to the TMR model. Based on this representation, for each conclusion, the SPARQL queries for strategy 1 are applied and combined to obtain the query pattern QP3 (conjunction of action and effect). The following is obtained for conclusion 5_1: *(breast reconstruction+mastectomy)+AND+((aesthetic result)+OR+(psychosocial wellbeing))*. However, alternative descriptions can be provided to the original terms. For example, the original composed action, described as "*Breast reconstruction immediately after mastectomy*", can be (re)interpreted as one action named "*primary breast reconstruction*" according to the vocabulary used in other conclusions of the same guideline.

```
#Conclusion 5_1 - divided in two sub-conclusions
2 data:CB-PrimaryBreastReconstruction-SatisfactionAppearance-WellBeing {
     data:CB-PrimaryBreastReconstruction-SatisfactionAppearance-WellBeing
4      rdf:type          tmr:CausationBelief ;
       tmr:conclusionID  "5_1";
6      tmr:hasPart       data:CB-PrimaryBC-SatAppearance, data:CB-PrimaryBC-WellBeing.}
   # One of the sub-conclusions, about causing higher satisfaction with appearance
8 data:CB-PrimaryBC-SatAppearance {
     data:CB-PrimaryBC-SatAppearance
10     rdf:type          tmr:CausationBelief .
     data:ActBC2004-BreastReconstructionImediatellyAfterMastectomy
12     tmr:causes        data:TrBC2004-HigherSatisfactionWithBreastAppearance.}
   # Composed extracted action
14 data:ActBC2004-BreastReconstructionImediatellyAfterMastectomy
       rdf:type          tmr:ActionType, tmr:ComposedEvent;
16     tmr:hasPart       data:ActBC2004-BreastReconstruction, data:ActBC2004-Mastectomy.
   # One of the sub-actions
18 data:ActBC2004-BreastReconstruction
       rdf:type          tmr:ActionType ;
20     rdfs:label        "breast reconstruction"@en .
   # One of the transtions (effect)
22 data:TrBC2004-HigherSatisfactionWithBreastAppearance
       rdf:type          tmr:TransitionType ;
24     tmr:affects       data:TropeBC2004-AestheticResult.
   # Property affected by the transition
26 data:TropeBC2004-AestheticResult
       rdf:type          tmr:TropeType;
28     rdfs:label        "aesthetic result"@en.
```

Listing 1.2. RDF code for conclusion 5_1 from Dutch Breast Cancer Guideline.

```
   # Link for original action resource with the reinterpreted one
2 data:ActBC2004-BreastReconstructionImediatellyAfterMastectomy
       tmr:interpretedAs  data:ActPrimaryBreastReconstruction.
4  # Reinterpretation for the aforementioned extracted action
   data:ActPrimaryBreastReconstruction
6      rdf:type          tmr:ActionType ;
       rdfs:label        "Primary Breast Reconstruction"@en .
```

Listing 1.3. RDF code for enriching terms from conclusion 5_1.

The Listing 1.3 presents the RDF representation of the aforementioned alternative description according to the TMR model: the resource corresponding to the composed action extracted from the guidelines, namely data:ActBC2004-

BreastReconstructionImediatellyAfterMastectomy is linked to another resource data:ActPrimaryBreastReconstruction via predicate tmr:interpretedAs. The latter resource, in turn, has the alternative description defined via rdfs:label predicate. For each conclusion, some alternative descriptions are provided based on: similar descriptions in other conclusions, descriptions provided by UMLS vocabulary, and finally some were based on the Mesh description obtained in the analysis.

Again, by applying the SPARQL queries for strategy 2 according to query pattern QP3, and given a number of alternative descriptions, the following query is obtained for conclusion 5_1: *(((Breast Reconstruction+Mastectomy)+OR+(Primary Breast Reconstruction)+OR+(Immediate Breast Reconstruction)))+AND+((Depression)+OR+ (Psychosocial Wellbeing)+OR+(Esthetics)+OR+(Body Image)+OR+(Cosmetic Result of Breast) +OR+(Breast Aesthetics)+OR+(Breast Appearance)+OR+(Quality Breast Appearance)).* The results are presented and discussed in the next section.

5.2 Results and Analysis

The results for both TMR-strategies 1 and 2 are presented in Table 2, together with the results obtained in previous text-based experiments [3]. For each conclusion we present the recall based on the goal evidence list (2/5 means 2 out of 5). The best recall results compared to the strategy right before are highlighted in the table (as Semantic Distance is the first, we highlight the better results compared to the TMR-1). In particular, some of the conclusions for which no results were obtained by using the Semantic Distance approaches are highlighted in bold (namely, 3_1, 3_3, 5_1, 7_1). Precision is not calculated since the goal list does not comprise all the possibly relevant papers but the ones indeed used in the updated version of the guideline. Calculating the precision requires

Table 2. Results obtained for experiment according to the method here proposed (strategies 1 and 2) and the previous Topic-Centric method described in Sect. 2.

Concl.	Semantic Distance			TMR-Strategy 1			TMR-Strategy 2		
	Recall	# Papers	Cost	Recall	# Papers	Cost	Recall	# Papers	Cost
1_1	2/5	60	30	1/5	110	110	3/5	2153	718
1_3	1/4	36	36	2/4	36	18	4/4	582	145
3_1	0/14	49	98	0/14	555	1110	8/14	1957	245
3_2	1/2	28	28	1/2	126	126	2/2	688	344
3_3	0/2	33	66	1/2	424	424	2/2	1418	709
4_1	3/5	1628	543	2/5	276	138	2/5	155	77
5_1	0/3	82	164	0/3	231	462	2/3	1130	565
6_1.1	5/5	9911	1982	0/5	12	24	5/5	540	108
6_1.2				0/5	8	16	2/5	298	149
6_2	1/3	72	72	1/3	53	53	2/3	427	213
7_1	0/2	372	744	1/2	48	48	2/2	97	48
8_1	1/2	324	324	2/2	535	267	2/2	295	147
AVG.	32.6%	1145.18	372	35.8%	221.18	254	80.9%	885.45	297

an expert to evaluate the relevance of all retrieved papers. Instead, we present the total number of papers retrieved (# Papers), and for the purpose of helping comparing the approaches, we compute a 'cost' regarding number of retrieved papers per hitted goal (when the number of hitted goals is zero, we multiply the number of retrieved papers per two as a simplification, considering a division per zero would be infinite cost). The average recall increases from 32.6% (Sem. Dist.) to 35.8% (TMR-1) and to 80.9% (TMR-2), while the average cost reduce from 372 (Sem. Dist.) to 254 (TMR-1) and then increase a bit to 297 (TMR-2).

Figure 4 shows on the left hand side the recall for each approach grouped per conclusion, while on the right hand side a complementary vision depicts the recall results in ascending order. This means that the x-axis does not identify the same conclusions anymore. For example, the first four results for Semantic Distance corresponds to conclusions 3_1, 3_3, 5_1 and 7_1 where recall is zero, while the first three results for TMR-1 corresponds to conclusions 3_1, 6_1 and 7_1 where recall is zero, and the first result for TMR-2 correspond to 4_1 where

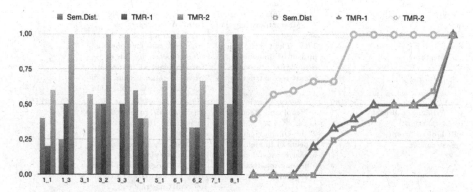

Fig. 4. Left hand side shows the recall for each approach grouped per conclusion. Right hand side depicts the same results in ascending order.

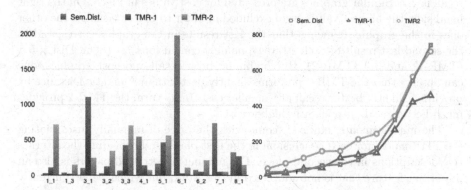

Fig. 5. Left hand side shows the cost for each approach grouped per conclusion. Right hand side depicts the results in ascending order, excluding the highest values.

Table 3. Part of the analysis of missing goals based on results of TMR-strategy 1. Divergences are **S**ynonyms, **R**elated concepts, **O**mitted terms, omitted **P**arts of term.

Concl./Terms	Goal	Mesh terms/Title	Reason/Divergence (S,R,O,P)	
3_1 - Breast-conserving therapy - Irradiation - Survival rate	1627428	- Mastectomy, Segmental - Breast Neoplasms/radiotherapy - Survival Rate	*Breast conserving therapy* can be **interpreted as** *Mastectomy, Segmental*	(S)
	12812844	- Mastectomy, Segmental - Breast Neoplasms/radiotherapy - Survival Analysis	*Survival Rate* **is related to** *Survival Analysis* (besides the same as line 1)	(R)
	15894097	- Survival Rate - Breast Neoplasms/therapy	The actions are **not mentioned**, or are mentioned as a **broader category**, namely *Breast Neoplasm Therapy*	(O) or (R)
	11355595	- Mastectomy, Segmental - Breast Neoplasms/radiotherapy	The effect is **not mentioned**	(O)
5_1 - Aesthetic result - Psychosocial wellbeing - Breast reconstruction - Mastectomy	10718173	- Body Image - Depression - Mammaplasty/methods - Mastectomy/psychology Title: The psychological impact of immediate rather than delayed breast reconstruction.	(1) *aesthetic result* **is related to** *Body Image* (2) *psychosocial wellbeing* **is related to** *Depression* (3) The composition *breast reconstruction immediately after mastectomy* can be **interpreted as** immediate breast reconstruction, as in the title of this publication	(S) and (R)
6_1.1 - Primary breast reconstruction - Risk of recurrent breast cancer	2545180	- Surgery, Plastic - Neoplasm Recurrence, Local Title: Oncological aspects of immediate breast reconstruction following mastectomy for malignancy.	(1) *Primary Breast Reconstruction* **is interpreted as** *Immediate Breast Reconstruction* (2) *risk of recurrent breast cancer* **is related to** *Neoplasm Recurrence*, because they are actually synonyms by omitting 'risk of'	(S) and (P)

recall is 2/5. Similar graphics are presented for cost values in Fig. 5. On the right hand side, the highest values were excluded in order to better visualise the other ones in the graphic. It means that the last results in the graphic correspond to the second last result of each strategy, namely conclusions 7_1 (Sem. Dist.), 5_1 (TMR-1) and 3_3 (TMR-2). By combining both recall and cost graphics, one can observe that the TMR-1 performs slightly better than Semantic Distance by providing slightly better recall at a smaller cost. In its turn, the TMR-2 provides much better recall at a slightly higher cost.

The improvements, however, come with the price of manually instantiating the TMR model for each conclusion, in the first place, and providing the alternative descriptions in the second place. The number of retrieved papers is also an important feature that is not addressed in this work, but which we are currently investigating, e.g. selecting the high quality publications. Ranking and filtering strategies are particularly important when more alternative terms are provided, specially using more flexible mechanisms such as related terms.

Another interesting result is the analysis of the missing goals (goal papers not retrieved by TMR-strategy 1) aimed at understanding the limitations of text-based querying PubMed and the possibilities of overcoming them by exploring the TMR model. Table 3 illustrates the analysis by presenting for three conclusions the original query terms, the PubMed-ID of some missing goals, some related Mesh terms and Title provided by PubMed for each goal, and finally a description of possible reasons why that goal was not retrieved and the type(s) of divergence. The divergences, annotated in the last column of the table, are due to: (S) low coverage of Synonyms, particularly when a composed action has itself a description; (R) some terms are described more generically, more specifically or by Related concepts; (O) some terms are Omitted; (P) some Parts of terms are omitted (e.g. *risk of*). By manually addressing some of the divergences, TMR-2 allows for providing better recall with respect to TMR-1, even though the results are biased.

6   Discussion

The results show that TMR-1 performed at least as good as Semantic Distance and TMR-2 performed much better at a not much higher 'reading cost' but much higher 'human-intervention cost'. We conclude that a knowledge-driven approach based on the TMR model allows for improving the recall with respect to previous experiments regarding the Dutch Breast Cancer guidelines, as the causation structure suggests important terms to be queried, namely action and effect. Through the analysis of the missing goal-evidences after an initial experiment, we show that richer ways to describe the medical terms (e.g. richer synonym coverage) besides more flexible search strategies (e.g. only actions or broader categories) are important features for searching relevant new evidences. In future work we will investigate if this holds for guidelines in general by performing experiments on other guidelines.

Although the alternative descriptions provided in our experiment can be considered biased towards the pre-defined goal evidences, we can conclude that the approach is expressive and flexible enough to allow for the adaptations required to retrieve the missing goals. The challenge is then what adaptations to do since the real problem does not provide a gold standard. We will investigate a semi-automated strategy for providing alternative descriptions based on controlled vocabularies such as UMLS or the conclusions' evidences. A text-based related work [8] do explore the CG evidences for retrieving new evidences from PubMed.

Two trade-offs are observed in this work and/or related ones [1–3,8]: fully automatic (text-based) *versus* manual (knowledge-driven) approach, as well as recall *versus* precision importance. In particular, the main difference between our previous approaches [2,3] and the current one is the selection of terms for constructing the term-queries (it can be seen from Figs. 1 and 3). The fully automatic semantic distance method is replaced by a knowledge-driven human intervention method. As expected, although the results are improved, the cost related to human intervention definitely increases. As we believe a middle term can be a suitable solution, we plan to pursue both (i) a semi-automated strategy for instantiating the TMR-model by using NLP and (ii) an interactive strategy that allows the experts to narrow down the results to the more relevant papers. Finally we will improve the model adding information potentially relevant for this task, such as link to evidences, risk factors and intervention comparison.

According to [9], current methodological books for guideline update do not provide formal explicit procedures for assessing the need for update. The authors refer to the use of terms dynamic updating and living guideline to suggest that guidelines are updated promptly and are always up-to-date, such as [10]. This regards more methodological than technological improvement, which would allow the responsible committee to update parts of the guideline more often, re-publishing it online and raising awareness of eventual updates. From a more computer science perspective, [11] already pointed to the need for a change in paradigm on the guideline authoring by adopting a modular structure so that parts of the guideline could be updated independently but also computer tools should support the living aspect of guidelines. Indeed, [12] claims that partial update of guidelines make more sense than updating the whole guideline at once and [13] does implement new paradigm for digital modular guideline authoring. However, to the best of our knowledge, systems to support 'living guideline' are being investigated, but still do not exist. Since our approach is also modular and the new evidence is retrieved per conclusion, which in turn is related to a recommendation, it would be a natural extension to point which part of the guideline can be updated considering the new evidence retrieved.

A follow-up challenge is to suggest what exactly need to be updated, why and where in the guideline given what has changed in the new evidence with respect to the current evidence. This is in line with the idea of computer-supported dynamic updating' and living guideline', but it requires the new evidence to be provided in a structured way, rather than in natural language. Some reasons for update are summarized in [14]: "(i) changes in available interventions; (ii) changes in evidence on the benefits and harms of existing interventions; (iii) changes in outcomes that are considered to be important; (iv) changes in evidence that current practice is optimal; (v) changes in values placed on outcomes; and (vi) changes in resources available for health care". Moreover, the existence of higher quality evidence can be identified by using approaches such as [15] that calculates the evidence quality by analyzing the meta-data provided by PubMed.

Despite to the lack of precise guidance aforementioned, [14] advocates that "several reputable guideline producers base the need to update on systematic literature searches that focus on some or all of the PICO questions from the original guideline". The PICO model means: **P**opulation, **I**ntervention, **C**omparison and **O**utcome. The authors of [16,17] advocate that automatically identifying the PICO elements for a query is very hard. However, given a PICO query (i.e. a query in which the elements are annotated according the PICO model), the obtained papers can be ranked based on a score attributed to the PICO elements and their matching against semi-automated detection of PICO elements in paper's abstract. As expected, similar, broader or narrower elements are considered to 'expand' the original ones. Moreover, [16] highlights that the PICO model specifies the different roles of the elements in a query, and that this should be considered to thoroughly balance elements in the ranking function.

This is in line with various positions advocated in this paper: (i) the need for a semi-automated extraction of the TMR elements, as for the PICO elements, given the difficulties to guarantee correctness in automatic extraction; (ii) that terms have different roles in a conclusion (actions and effects) and therefore are composed differently into the query (see Sect. 3), such as for the PICO-based ranking; (iii) the need to 'expand' the original terms with related terms (TMR Strategy-2); and (iv) that precision measurement can be reconsidered by interactive ranking and filtering strategies. Finally, the PICO model partially aligns with the TMR model (actions $\cong$ intervention and effect $\cong$ outcome). Therefore we advocate our approach can be extended for supporting the elaboration of queries based on the PICO model. Further investigation is needed to extend the approach to consider Population and Comparison when composing the query.

7 Conclusion

This work analyses the information retrieval problem for supporting Clinical Guidelines update tasks. Part of the TMR-model is presented for structuring Clinical Guidelines' conclusions. The structured information is then used to design a new knowledge-driven approach for retrieving relevant scientific publication from the PubMed repository. The contribution is on the method to automatically generate PubMed queries using as input the clinical guidelines conclusions represented according to the TMR model. The implemented experiments evaluate the performance of the knowledge-driven approach for supporting the updating task of the Dutch Breast Cancer Guideline. First, an older version of the guideline is used to extract the conclusions and to formalise it according to the TMR model. Then, the list of scientific papers used to update the guideline, named goal evidences, is obtained from its latest version. Finally, PubMed queries are automatically generated per conclusion according to the proposed method, and are further submitted to PubMed API to retrieve a list of publications for each conclusion in the guideline. The resultant list is checked against the goal evidences. The performance of the proposed approach is compared with previous experiment, showing that the performance can be improved when using knowledge-driven strategies. Although the good performance observed, the proposed approach has a cost: human intervention is required to formalise the free-text guideline-conclusions according to TMR model and to enrich it with alternative descriptions. The weakness of the model is the limited type of information that it can represent, e.g. risk factor is not yet covered. We are working on improvements in the model, in the query elaboration and in the evaluation process to reach better performance. We also aim at reducing human intervention.

References

1. Reinders, R., ten Teije, A., Huang, Z.: Finding evidence for updates in medical guideline. In: Proceedings of HEALTHINF 2015, Lisbon (2015)
2. Hu, Q., Huang, Z., ten Teije, A., van Harmelen, F.: Detecting new evidence for evidence-based guidelines using a semantic distance method. In: Proceedings of the 15th Conference on Artificial Intelligence in Medicine (AIME 2015) (2015)
3. Hu, Q., Huang, Z., ten Teije, A., van Harmelen, F., Marshall, M., Dekker, A.: A topic-centric approach to detecting new evidences for evidence-based medical guidelines. In: Proceedings of HEALTHINF 2016, Rome (2016)
4. Zamborlini, V., Hoekstra, R., Silveira, M., Pruski, C., Teije, A.: Generalizing the detection of internal and external interactions in clinical guidelines. In: Proceedings of the 9th International Conference on Health Informatics (HEALTHINF 2016), Rome, Italy (2016)
5. NABON: Guideline for the treatment of breast carcinoma 2004. Technical report, Nationaal Borstkanker Overleg Nederland (NABON) (2004)
6. NABON: Breast cancer, dutch guideline, version 2.0. Technical report, Integraal kankercentrum Netherland, Nationaal Borstkanker Overleg Nederland (2012)
7. Zamborlini, V., da Silveira, M., Pruski, C., ten Teije, A., van Harmelen, F.: Analyzing recommendations interactions in clinical guidelines: impact of action type hierarchies and causation beliefs. In: AI in Medicine (AIME 2015), pp. 317–326 (2015)
8. Iruetaguena, A., Adeva, J.G., Pikatza, J., Segundo, U., Buenestado, D., Barrena, R.: Automatic retrieval of current evidence to support update of bibliography in clinical guidelines. Expert Syst. Appl. 40, 2081–2091 (2013)
9. Vernooij, R.W.M., Sanabria, A.J., Sola, I., Alonso-Coello, P., Martinez Garcia, L.: Guidance for updating clinical practice guidelines: a systematic review of methodological handbooks. Implementation Sci. IS 9(1), 3 (2014)
10. SIGN: British guideline on the management of asthma. A clinical national guideline, British Thoracic Society (2005)
11. ten Teije, A., Marcos, M., Balser, M., van Croonenborg, J., Duelli, C., Van Harmelen, F., Lucas, P., Miksch, S., Reif, W., Rosenbrand, K., Seyfang, A.: Improving medical protocols by formal methods. AI Med. 36(3), 193–209 (2006)
12. Becker, M., Neugebauer, E.A., Eikermann, M.: Partial updating of clinical practice guidelines often makes more sense than full updating: a systematic review on methods and the development of an updating procedure. J. Clin. Epidemiol. 67(1), 33–45 (2014)
13. Vandvik, P.O., Brandt, L., Alonso-Coello, P., Treweek, S., Akl, E.A., Kristiansen, A., Fog-Heen, A., Agoritsas, T., Montori, V.M., Guyatt, G.: Creating clinical practice guidelines we can trust, use, and share a new era is imminent (2013)
14. Uhlig, K., Berns, J.S., Carville, S., Chan, W., Cheung, M., Guyatt, G.H., Hart, A., Lewis, S.Z., Tonelli, M., Webster, A.C., Wilt, T.J., Kasiske, B.L.: Recommendations for kidney disease guideline updating: a report by the KDIGO Methods Committee (2016)
15. Huang, Z., Hu, Q., Teije, A., Harmelen, F.: Identifying evidence quality for updating evidence-based medical guidelines. In: Riaño, D., Lenz, R., Miksch, S., Peleg, M., Reichert, M., Teije, A. (eds.) KR4HC 2015. LNCS (LNAI), vol. 9485, pp. 51–64. Springer, Cham (2015). doi:10.1007/978-3-319-26585-8_4

16. Boudin, F., Nie, J.Y., Dawes, M.: Clinical information retrieval using document and PICO structure. In: Proceedings of the 21st International Conference on Computational Linguistics and 44th Annual Meeting of the Association for Computational Linguistics, Association for Computational Linguistics, pp. 822–830 (2006)

17. Znaidi, E., Tamine, L., Latiri, C.: Answering PICO clinical questions: a semantic graph-based approach. In: Holmes, J.H., Bellazzi, R., Sacchi, L., Peek, N. (eds.) AIME 2015. LNCS (LNAI), vol. 9105, pp. 232–237. Springer, Cham (2015). doi:10.1007/978-3-319-19551-3_30

Applying SPARQL-Based Inference and Ontologies for Modelling and Execution of Clinical Practice Guidelines: A Case Study on Hypertension Management

Charalampos Doulaverakis[1]([✉]), Vassilis Koutkias[2], Grigoris Antoniou[1], and Ioannis Kompatsiaris[3]

[1] Department of Informatics, University of Huddersfield,
Huddersfield, UK
{charalampos.doulaverakis,g.antoniou}@hud.ac.uk
[2] Centre for Research and Technology Hellas,
Institute of Applied Biosciences, Thessaloniki, Greece
vkoutkias@certh.gr
[3] Centre for Research and Technology Hellas,
Information Technologies Institute, Thessaloniki, Greece
ikom@iti.gr

Abstract. Clinical practice guidelines (CPGs) constitute a systematically developed, critical body of medical knowledge which is compiled and maintained in order to assist healthcare professionals in decision making. They are available for diverse diseases/conditions and routinely used in many countries, providing reference material for healthcare delivery in clinical settings. As CPGs are paper-based, i.e. plain documents, there have been various approaches for their computerization and expression in a formal manner so that they can be incorporated in clinical information and decision support systems. Semantic Web technologies and ontologies have been extensively used for CPG formalization. In this paper, we present a novel method for the representation and execution of CPGs using OWL ontologies and SPARQL-based inference rules. The proposed approach is capable of expressing complex CPG constructs and can be used to express formalisms, such as negations, which are hard to express using ontologies alone. The encapsulation of SPARQL rules in the CPG ontology is based on the SPARQL Inference Notation (SPIN). The proposed representation of different aspects of CPGs, such as numerical comparisons, calculations, decision branches and state transitions, and their execution is demonstrated through the respective parts of comprehensive, though complex enough, CPGs for arterial hypertension management. The paper concludes by comparing the proposed approach with other relevant works, indicating its potential and limitations, as well as a future work directions.

Keywords: Clinical practice guidelines (CPG) · CPG modelling and representation · Ontologies · Semantic Web · SPARQL Inference Notation (SPIN) · Hypertension management

© Springer International Publishing AG 2017
D. Riaño et al. (Eds.): KR4HC/ProHealth 2016, LNAI 10096, pp. 90–107, 2017.
DOI: 10.1007/978-3-319-55014-5_6

1   Introduction

Clinical practice guidelines (CPGs) are an integral part of healthcare delivery, aiming to reinforce quality of care and standardization of treatment [1]. Various studies have illustrated the benefits of CPG adoption in medical practice, such as reduction of practice variability and patient care costs, as well as better and safer patient care [2–4]. CPGs vary according to the application domain as well as the scope of use (diagnosis, treatment, follow-up, etc.). They are typically provided as textual recommendations (traditionally in paper-based format, but lately also as electronic documents available through the Internet). CPGs result from a systematic and intensive procedure conducted by groups of qualified medical experts (both regarding their development and maintenance) [5], under the auspices or upon request of scientific authorities (e.g. expert medical societies) and national/international health institutions.

Despite the benefits, various difficulties hamper the widespread development and implementation of CPGs in clinical practice. For example, long text-based documents are cumbersome to read as well as difficult to integrate and apply in the patient care process, while maintenance (e.g., updating and versioning [6]) and (local) adaptation (e.g., adapting national guidelines to local protocols) require significant resources and a methodological framework as well [7]. On another strand, healthcare institutions pay more attention to guideline development than to guideline implementation for routine use in daily care.

It has been argued that challenges such as the above can be addressed by representing CPGs via formal, computer-interpretable formats [8]. To this end, various approaches have been proposed for CPG formalization. In this paper, we present a new approach for representing and executing CPGs using Web Ontology Language (OWL) ontologies [9] and SPARQL-based inference rules [10]. The approach supports the expression and execution of complex CPG constructs, such as negations, which are hard to express using ontologies alone [11], as well as numerical comparisons, calculations, decision branches and state transitions. The encapsulation of SPARQL rules in the CPG ontology is based on the SPARQL Inference Notation (SPIN)[1] which provides an open framework for defining and executing inference rules. Our approach was evaluated in two CPGs concerning arterial hypertension as illustrated in the paper.

The paper is structured as follows: In Sect. 2 we provide background information on computer interpretable CPGs and their execution. Section 3 presents the selected use case and the requirements that have been identified. Section 4 describes the methodological approach for representing and executing CPGs via Semantic Web standards and SPARQL-based inference and in Sect. 5 we present some early evaluation results. In Sect. 6 we discuss our contribution by comparing it with relevant works and indicating its potential, limitations, as well as future work directions, while Sect. 7 concludes the paper.

---

[1] SPARQL Inference Notation, http://spinrdf.org/.

2　Background

Representation of CPGs in computer-interpretable format has been a very active field of research. For an overview of diverse efforts and formats, we refer the reader to the review papers of Peleg [8], Wang et al. [12], Latoszek-Berendsen et al. [13] and De Clercq et al. [14], while a comprehensive comparative study on six (widely known) of these formats has been presented by Peleg et al. [15]. Models such as GLIF (Guideline Interchange Format) [16], PROforma [17] and Asbru [18] have been systematically developed for years. The emphasis was given on providing appropriate CPG representations that would enable their sharing across institutions or across different types of applications within an institution, by addressing the differences met in: (a) formats used to represent guideline knowledge, (b) data models and terminologies used within the encoded guidelines, and (c) clinical information systems with which they are integrated [16].

Formal representations of CPGs may reinforce their comprehension by healthcare professionals, as well as their exploitation by healthcare IT systems [19], such as Clinical Decision Support Systems (CDSSs) and Computerized Physician Order Entry (CPOE) systems. To this end, another important aspect in the domain of computer-interpretable CPGs, which is implicitly linked with their representation, concerns their computer-based execution. An interesting review on computer-based execution of CPGs has been presented by Isern and Moreno [20]. Execution brings in the forefront issues such as consistency checking [21], verification [22], traceability [23], decidability [24], as well as performance and robustness [25], which shall be addressed when exploiting computer-interpretable CPGs in practice. These issues are linked with the application per se (e.g. consultation-advice dialogue applications, event-driven alerts/reminders, quality monitoring and assessment, constraint-checking in CPOE systems, etc.), posing diverse functional requirements (e.g. response time constraints), which led in many times to the design of application-specific languages.

Recently, Semantic Web technologies have been employed for representing and executing computer-interpretable CPGs, aiming to overcome barriers, such as shareability and machine processability. Semantic Web technologies address these barriers thanks to standardization and the flexibility offered through various tools that become available. Interestingly, a recent study by Jafarpour et al. demonstrated the potential of three CPG execution engines based on OWL 1 DL, OWL 2 DL and OWL 2 DL combined with Semantic Web Rule Language (SWRL) [26]. The idea was to overcome the lack of ability to execute CPG with high levels of expressivity while overcoming the cognitive load of computerizing paper-based CPGs and facilitating the update of computerized versions. These engines were proven capable of executing more complex CPGs compared to other Semantic Web reasoning-based CPG execution engines. The study also highlighted the shortcoming in representing and reasoning temporal constraints in CPGs, as well as the potential to utilize other types of formal languages, e.g. Petri nets.

In order to define a methodology for expressing computerized CPGs using Semantic Web technologies in a simple manner for efficient CPG execution, several issues should be considered. These are: (a) the expressions and the execution engine should be able to handle numerical data, (b) the framework should be able to handle negation in order to efficiently handle expression such as "a patient's medication plan does not include drug A", (c) new facts should be able to be inserted, in order to simplify expressions and execution; although this would lead to a non-monotonic system, the benefit of simpler expressions is more important, as it allows easier computer interpretable CPG construction. While the above issues have been successfully addressed using OWL reasoning and rule languages such as SWRL [26,27], the solutions that were employed resulted in complex ontological definitions and, in some cases, in ad-hoc solutions for the expression of execution semantics, while also being computationally expensive and requiring a rather large amount of time for execution.

To this end, the current study elaborated further on the adoption of Semantic Web technologies for representing CPGs, combining OWL with SPARQL-based inference rules. SPARQL introduces features such as the generation of graph patterns, aggregate functions, filtering and negation support that allow the definition of not only complex queries but also the generation of triples that can enrich a repository[2]. The outcome is a methodology for expressing various aspects of CPGs in a standardized manner, while also allowing computationally efficient inference and rule execution. The proposed approach in presented in detail in the following sections.

3   Case Study and Requirements

3.1   Case Study

In the scope of the current study, we elaborated on representing and executing the 2013 guidelines released by the European Society of Hypertension (ESH) and the European Society of Cardiology (ESC) for the management of arterial hypertension [28] and the guidelines published by the 8th Joint National Committee (JNC8) [29]. These CPGs were selected due to: (a) the importance and wide applicability of hypertension management in the healthcare domain, (b) their comprehensive and detailed description, but also (c) the encapsulation of a wide variety of CPG constructs introducing diverse knowledge representation challenges (e.g. numerical comparisons, calculations, expressions, decision branches and state transitions) that shall be addressed via the proposed approach. Briefly, the considered CPGs are broad enough, covering diagnosis, treatment approaches and strategies (accounting also for special conditions and associated risk factors), as well as follow-up.

While we focused on these specific CPGs, these were considered as adequate examples for a proof-of-concept modelling and implementation study exploiting the proposed approach.

---

[2] SPARQL CONSTRUCT, http://www.w3.org/TR/rdf-sparql-query/#construct.

3.2 Requirements

An important part of CPG execution involves data-based inference, i.e. being able to perform actions based on data values. Data-based inference facilitates actions such as the generation of new data and knowledge, decision making (e.g. ending the execution of a CPG when certain numerical criteria have been met), or control flow execution. Based on the analysis that was performed on the CPGs that were mentioned in Sect. 3.1, a number of requirements for CPG execution have been identified, which are presented below. Overall three requirements have been defined pertaining to data-based inference, while one is relevant with control flow of CPGs. Although these requirements cannot be considered exhaustive for CPG execution, they are quite generic and were the driving elements for the proposed methodology.

R1 Numerical expressions. The ability to represent expressions on numerical input that are usually applied on patient data and can be as simple as age calculation or more complex, such as the calculation of Body Mass Index (BMI), that require mathematical operations on the data.

R2 Comparison of patient data with predefined values. This is one of the most obvious requirements and exploits patient data. It corresponds to various stages of the CPG execution such as for determining the risk factors of a patient (based e.g. on laboratory examination results, age, sex, etc.) or decision branches during workflow execution.

R3 Expressions for condition satisfaction. This requirement involves the ability to define more complex expressions than in R2 as these not only exploit patient data but also take as input previous inferred results and operate on them to derive new knowledge. An example of such an expression is the addition of previously derived risk factors for patient risk stratification.

R4 State transitions for monitoring guideline execution. This is an important requirement for guideline execution in order to be able to figure out which part of the guideline the current execution process has reached and what are the possible paths to follow. State knowledge and state transition should be fully supported by the execution engine. For state transition, the execution engine relies on data that are either explicitly available or have been inferred according to the previously defined CPG aspects and follow the correct execution path.

While one could argue that some of the requirements are overlapping, e.g. R2 and R3 both operate on data, this categorization was followed to emphasize the different operations that should be supported in CPG execution. In the current work, the rules expressed to address R3 utilize different features of SPARQL, i.e. aggregate functions, compared to the rules for addressing R2 (FILTER expressions). In the remainder of the paper, these requirements will be addressed according to the given numbering, R1–R4.

4   Approach and Methodology

For representing a CPG, an ontology that will encode the structure and semantics of constructs such as Decisions, Tasks, Branches, Actions has to be defined. Based on these definitions, rules for enabling inference and flow control are specified. The proposed approach makes use and extends a CPG core ontology that is defined from previous works and utilizes a novel methodology for rule expression and execution using a SPARQL-based inference framework.

4.1   Ontology

The ontology proposed in [30] has been used as the baseline, adapted for the purpose of our work. An overview of the ontology along with the concepts that have been added is displayed in Fig. 1 where the concepts that are used to describe the workflow (algorithm) for managing hypertension can be seen, as specified in [29]. Besides the definition of new classes, for concepts such as *Patient* and *LabTest*, several additions have been made in order to be able to easily represent the workflow during CPG execution. Each task, e.g. an *Action* or a *Decision*, is followed by another task through the *HasNextStep* property. A *Decision* task is comprised of two or more *DecisionBranches* and each branch is followed by other tasks. A similar representation has also been used in the SDA language where a guideline is analyzed as a flowchart composed of States, Decisions and Actions [31].

Using such an approach, it is possible to navigate through the guideline using the ontology alone which also makes it easier to compose the conditions and rules for state transitions in guideline execution, as elaborated later in the paper.

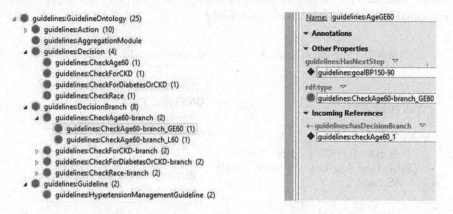

Fig. 1. Part of the ontology defined incorporating concepts for the Management of Arterial Hypertension CPG [29]

4.2   SPARQL-Based Inference

For CPG expression, SPARQL rules are utilized that encode the various expressions contained in the CPGs. The selection of SPARQL-based inference for guideline expression was made for a number of reasons, with the main ones being that (a) SPARQL rules support closed world reasoning with the use of the FILTER NOT EXISTS construct, (b) new facts can be asserted using the SPARQL CONSTRUCT expression, (c) SPARQL UPDATE can be used for updating data in the knowledge base, (d) data constraints can easily be expressed and (e) evaluation and execution of SPARQL rules is computationally efficient and can produce results in an acceptable amount of time. SPARQL rules offer flexibility in rule expression and data manipulation, e.g. regarding the addition and deletion of facts, and have successfully been used for inference in other works such as in [32] for the recognition of high level events in context-aware pervasive environments.

In order to enable sharing and execution of the SPARQL rules, the SPIN framework has been employed. SPIN has been submitted as a W3C Recommendation for a SPARQL-based rule and constraint language[3] and provides the vocabulary and syntax for expressing these rules and integrate their expression in an ontology. As such, it enables the distribution of domain models (ontologies) along with rules and constraints for data validation and behaviour. It is an open source framework that includes the libraries for both expressing the rules and executing them.

4.3   Rule Definitions

As has been mentioned in Sect. 3, the proposed approach was applied to two widespread CPGs regarding Arterial Hypertension Management. In this section we will demonstrate the applicability of the approach and how the requirements described in Sect. 3.2 have been addressed.

Table 1. Numerical expressions: (a) calculate age, (b) calculate BMI

# Calculate age 	
CONSTRUCT {
    ?this gl:hasAge ?age .}
WHERE {
    ?this gl:hasBirthDate ?date .
    BIND (smf:duration("y", ?date, now())
        AS ?age) }
	# Calculate BMI
	CONSTRUCT {
	    ?this gl:hasBMI ?bmi .}
	WHERE {
	    ?this gl:hasHeight ?height .
	    ?this gl:hasWeight ?weight .
	    BIND ((?weight/(?height*?height))
	        AS ?bmi) }

(a)	(b)

---

[3] SPIN - Overview and Motivation, https://www.w3.org/Submission/2011/SUBM-spin-overview-20110222/.

Table 2. Risk factors assessment: (a) dyslipidaemia risk factor, (b) addition of risk factors

```
# Dyslipidemia risk factor
CONSTRUCT {
   ?this gl:hasRiskFactor gl:dyslipidemia_rf .}
WHERE {                                 # Count total risk factors
   OPTIONAL {                           CONSTRUCT {
      ?this gl:hasTotalCholesterol ?chol .     ?this gl:hasTotalRiskFactors ?tRF .}
      ?chol gl:hasUnitMeasure gl:mmolPerL . WHERE {
      ?chol gl:testHasValue ?value .        {SELECT ((COUNT(?rf))
      FILTER (?value > 4.9)                           AS ?tRF) ?this
   }                                          WHERE {
   OPTIONAL {                                    ?this gl:hasRiskFactor ?rf .
      ?this gl:hasLDL ?ldl .                  }
      ?ldl gl:hasUnitMeasure gl:mmolPerL .    GROUP BY ?this}}
      ?ldl gl:testHasValue ?value .
      FILTER (?value > 3.0)
}}
```

          (a)   (b)

In order to address requirement R1 (Numerical expressions), since SPIN supports the SPARQL 1.1 specification along with a number of convenience functions, expressions can be defined as in rule Table 1a which calculates a patient's age based on their birth date. The keyword *?this* used in SPIN instructs the rule engine to apply this rule on the instances of the class that the rule is attached to. The function *smf:duration* operates on date values and calculates the time span between a start and an end date. So attaching rule of Table 1a to the *Patient* class will calculate the age of the *Patient* instances of the ontology and insert the respective triple of the CONSTRUCT clause. Using rule language terminology, the CONSTRUCT clause is the head of the rule while the WHERE clause is the body of the rule. Similarly, a rule which would compute the BMI of a patient is displayed in rule Table 1b where a more complex expression is used. In both examples, the calculation is straightforward and simple to express. New data are directly persisted and can be exploited by subsequent rules.

Regarding requirement R2 (Comparison of patient data with predefined values), an example is given in [28] (Table 4, p. 2167) where patients are assigned risk factors for developing cardiovascular disease (CVD) based on biochemical test measurements or other facts. A particular one used for deciding on dyslipidaemia is rather complex and is illustrated in Table 3. It states that a patient has risk of developing CVD when total cholesterol is above 4.9 mmol/L −*AND/OR*− LDL cholesterol is more than 3.0 mmol/L −*AND/OR*− HDL cholesterol is less that 1.2 mmol/L for men 1.0 mmol/L for women −*AND/OR*− triglycerides are more than 1.7 mmol/L. These conditions can be observed independently (*OR*) or simultaneously (*AND*). *OR*'ed conditions can be expressed

Table 3. Assessment of dyslipidaemia risk factor. Dyslipidaemia is present if one or more of these conditions are met

Dyslipidaemia
Total cholesterol > 4.9 mmol/L (190 mg/dL)
LDL chol. > 3.0 mmol/L (115 mg/dL)
HDL chol. < 1.0 mmol/L (40 mg/dL), men or < 1.2 mmol/L (46 mg/dL), women
Triglycerides > 1.7 mmol/L (150 mg/dL)

using the OPTIONAL clause is SPARQL as in Table 2a (note that due to its length, only a part of the rule is presented).

Requirement R3 involves the definition of expressions for condition satisfaction. An example for such a requirement can be found in [28] (Fig. 1, p. 2166) where a table for patient risk stratification is given according to a combination of the number of risk factors that apply to them and other data taken from their medical record. In order to add the number of risk factors that have been determined, the rule of Table 2b is used which employs the aggregate COUNT defined in SPARQL 1.1.

The rules of Table 2 are attached to the *Patient* class so that they are automatically applied to its instances, implied by keyword *?this*, as has been mentioned earlier.

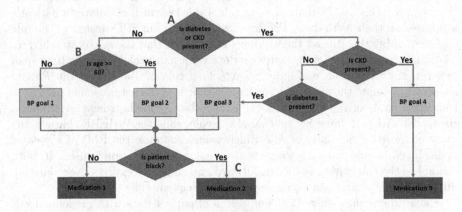

Fig. 2. Algorithm for Management of Arterial Hypertension CPG [29]. BP goal = Blood Pressure goal

Finally, addressing requirement R4 (State transition) is key for computerized CPG execution as it involves the execution of a workflow or "algorithm" of the guideline related e.g. to management, treatment or diagnosis of a disease. An example of such a workflow can be seen on [29] (Figure, p. 516). The execution of such an algorithm requires to be able to decide on the validity of the conditions that describe when a state should be reached and what execution path should be followed, based on the available data. The aforementioned algorithm is illustrated in Fig. 2. The algorithm runs as follows: The patient medical history is searched to determine if he/she suffers from diabetes or Chronic Kidney Disease (CKD), (State A in Fig. 2). If none is present. then the patient age is checked to see if he/she is older than 60 years old (State B). Depending on the age, different blood pressure (BP) target values are aimed. After the target BP is determined, the final check is to identify if the patient's race is black or non black. The appropriate medication that is then selected (State C).

In order to demonstrate how such a workflow would be expressed using SPARQL rules, Table 4 presents the state transition conditions from state A to B and from B to C in Fig. 2 where execution should apply the transition if the patient is not suffering from diabetes or chronic kidney disease (CKD) and if the patient is of black race. This example demonstrates the use of negation with the FILTER NOT EXISTS clause and the ability to update data using the SPARQL UPDATE's DELETE/INSERT operation. This example also demonstrates the ability of our approach to effectively support the procedural representation of a CPG where the decision to prescribe a certain medication is reached through branching.

Table 4. State transitions

```
# State transition A -> B
DELETE {?gl gl:hasExecutionState gl:checkForDiabetesOrCKD}
INSERT {?gl gl:hasExecutionState gl:checkAge60}
WHERE {
    ?gl gl:hasExecutionState gl:checkForDiabetesOrCKD .
    ?patient gl:patientExecutesGuideline ?gl .
    FILTER NOT EXISTS {
      ?patient gl:hasDisease ?disease .
      FILTER (?disease=gl:Diabetes || ?disease=gl:CKD)
} }
```

```
# State transition B -> C
DELETE {?gl gl:hasExecutionState gl:checkAge60}
INSERT {?gl gl:hasExecutionState gl:prescribeMedication2}
WHERE {
    ?gl gl:hasExecutionState gl:checkAge60 .
    ?patient gl:patientExecutesGuideline ?gl .
    ?patient gl:hasDisease ?disease .
    ?patient gl:race gl:black .
    }
```

5   Results

As a proof-of-concept implementation of the approach presented in Sect. 4, the
CPG rules were expressed in the development and testing environment of Top-
Braid Composer[4], a modelling environment supporting OWL inference and SPIN
rules. The ontology described in Sect. 4.1 was developed using Composer's environment and the rules presented in Sect. 4.3 were entered and attached to the
appropriate classes of the ontology. An illustration of the *Patient* class with
rules for calculating age, assigning age risk factor and counting the number of
risk factors for a patient is presented in Fig. 3.

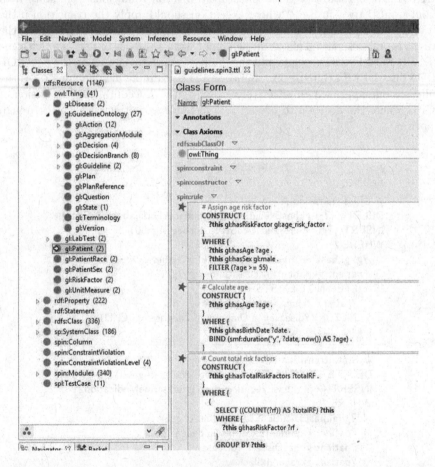

Fig. 3. Illustration of the Patient class with several rules attached to it in the development and testing environment of TopBraid Composer

---

[4]. TopBraid Composer, http://www.topquadrant.com/tools/modeling-topbraid-
composer-standard-edition/.

For testing the CPG execution, a number of *Patient* instances were created and inferences were obtained (OWL inference + SPARQL rules) in order to investigate the results. Figure 4 displays a patient instance where birth date, sex and laboratory examination result values (for total cholesterol) were inserted as facts. After running the inferences, additional facts regarding age, risk factors and total risk factors were asserted. Inferred facts are displayed over a light blue background. In a realistic scenario, for the execution of the guideline, a patient instance would be created automatically and data would be imported from the patient's medical record in to be semantically annotated. Thus the guideline is executed on a per-patient basis.

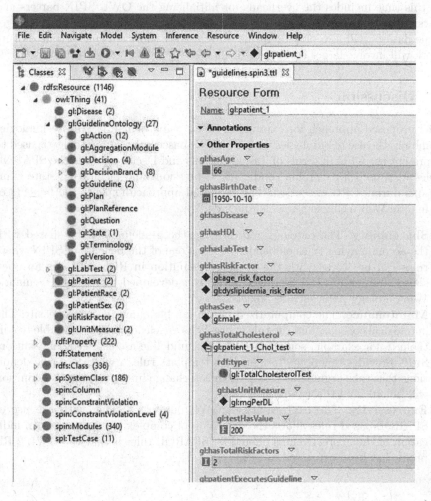

Fig. 4. Patient instance with defined and inferred facts (Color figure online)

Regarding the rules for state transitions, described under requirement R4, patient instances were created and relevant data were inserted as above. The rules for state transition were entered (States A, B, C in Fig. 2) and inferences were started. The execution state of the guideline was correctly updated successively from State A to State B and finally to State C. This is partially illustrated in Fig. 5 where Fig. 5a shows the initial state of the guideline (State A, check patient for the presence of CKD or diabetes) and Fig. 5b shows the final State C (prescribe medication) after inferences were evaluated.

Regarding execution time, this example in the TopBraid Composer's environment required 37 ms to be completed in a standard workstation (Intel Core i7 CPU with 16 GB of RAM running Windows 8.1). This is a satisfactory result as this time includes the overheads for initializing the OWL/SPIN parsers and parsing the ontology and rules. It is expected that an evaluation with a larger scale dataset will also provide results in relatively short amount of time. Future work will involve larger scale experiments.

6   Discussion

The proposed approach for expressing CPGs using Semantic Web technologies combines the use of ontologies with SPARQL-based rules. An ontology is used to represent the CPG in terms of Tasks, Actions and Decisions while the SPARQL rules were used for defining conditions, expressions and facilitating state transitions during CPG execution. The proposed approach exploits the benefits of Semantic Web technologies which include [26]:

- **Shareability.** The ontology representing the guideline can be shared with the accompanying rules embedded. This is one of the benefits of SPIN where rules can be stored with the ontology definition in RDF. SPIN is an open source framework and bindings have been developed for popular Semantic Web ontology APIs such as Apache Jena[5].
- **Maintenance.** The computerized CPGs can be maintained more easily. The ontological concepts and the rule expressions are clear enough to be able to edit them if, for example, some aspects of the guideline are changed. In addition, SPIN provides functionalities, such as template rules[6], which are rule definitions that take arguments as input, thus a change in the template's definition will be reflected throughout the CPG.
- **Expressivity.** The expressivity of OWL ontologies along with the use of SPARQL-based rules allows the definition of complex CPG aspects. An indication of the expressiveness offered by SPARQL rules is that the OWL 2 RL profile has been expressed in SPIN[7].

---

[5] Apache Jena, http://jena.apache.org.
[6] SPIN Templates, http://spinrdf.org/spin.html#spin-templates.
[7] SPIN OWL 2 RL profile, http://topbraid.org/spin/owlrl-all.html.

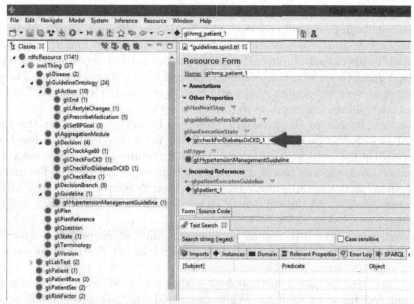

(a) Initial state of the guideline (indicated by the red arrow)

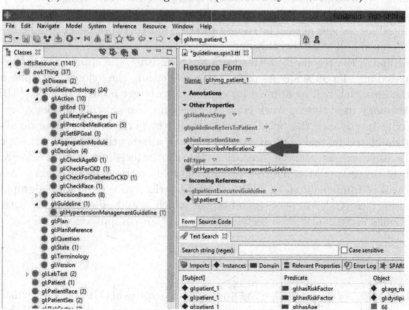

(b) Final state of the guideline after rules execution

Fig. 5. State transitions using SPARQL UPDATE rules (Color figure online)

In addition, while various approaches for computerized representation of CPGs have been proposed, each approach focuses on different aspects of guideline modelling and representation, and as such these have implications. Our approach fulfils the set of minimal requirements defined by de Clercq et al. [14], i.e.: (a) Support a set of generic guideline tasks that is able to represent all facets of simple as well as complex diagnostic and treatment guidelines. (b) Rely on formal control-flow languages as well as expression languages.

Another benefit of the approach presented in this paper is that the time needed in order to execute the CPG is short. While the evaluation has been performed in limited test cases, computational requirements are low since the semantics used are not complex and the execution of SPARQL rules makes full benefit of the optimizations that have been developed for the SPARQL language. As such, the time to deliver an answer, given the patient data and the computerized CPG, is short.

What hasn't been investigated is the applicability of the proposed approach for CPG formal analysis and validation. This might not be trivial to support as the approach relies on both ontologies and non DL-safe rule-based inference. In addition, the proposed methodology makes use of SPARQL UPDATE for deletion and insertion of facts. While one could argue that this could cause problems with valid inferences, deletion is restricted to state transition tracking in order to monitor the guideline execution and not for the inferences that are produced for patient data. The results showed that this approach proved efficient for inference and state monitoring.

Although the results from this work are promising, the approach needs to be evaluated on a larger scale. As part of this evaluation, the following are planned: (a) the approach will be applied for expressing a larger number of CPGs, (b) as the ontology used in this work is an adaptation of an existing ontology, we are planning to advance the ontology model and (c) perform an evaluation study on a simulated or real clinical dataset to have a indication of the performance of the approach in realistic scenarios. For the latter, linkage with Electronic Medical Records (EMR) in order to automatically retrieve the pertinent patient data will be implemented. In addition, a long-term goal is to develop a graphical user interface (GUI) to serve as an editor which would allow someone with no experience in Semantic Web technologies to author computerized CPGs.

7   Conclusions

In this paper, we presented a novel approach for expressing CPGs using Semantic Web technologies. The approach utilizes OWL ontologies and SPARQL-based rules and inference for providing the tools to express the various CPG aspects and perform CPG execution while the use of the SPIN framework allows the rules to be embedded in the ontology and efficiently executed. The approach was evaluated on two CPGs for Arterial Hypertension Management and proved its applicability. Further evaluations are planned, in order to obtain better insights on the approach's performance.

Acknowledgements. This work was supported by the projects MULTISENSOR (contract no. FP7-610411) and KRISTINA (contract no. H2020-645012), partially funded by the European Commission.

References

1. Field, M.J., Lohr, K.N., et al.: Guidelines for Clinical Practice: From Development to Use. National Academies Press (1992)
2. Eagle, K.A., Montoye, C.K., Riba, A.L., DeFranco, A.C., Parrish, R., Skorcz, S., Baker, P.L., Faul, J., Jani, S.M., Chen, B., et al.: Guideline-based standardized care is associated with substantially lower mortality in medicare patients with acute myocardial infarction: the American College of Cardiologys Guidelines Applied in Practice (GAP) Projects in Michigan. J. Am. Coll. Cardiol. **46**(7), 1242–1248 (2005)
3. Grimshaw, J.M., Russell, I.T.: Effect of clinical guidelines on medical practice: a systematic review of rigorous evaluations. Lancet **342**(8883), 1317–1322 (1993)
4. Damiani, G., Pinnarelli, L., Colosimo, S.C., Almiento, R., Sicuro, L., Galasso, R., Sommella, L., Ricciardi, W.: The effectiveness of computerized clinical guidelines in the process of care: a systematic review. BMC Health Serv. Res. **10**(1), 1 (2010)
5. Shekelle, P.G., Woolf, S.H., Eccles, M., Grimshaw, J.: Clinical guidelines: developing guidelines. Br. Med. J. **318**(7183), 593 (1999)
6. Kaiser, K., Miksch, S.: Versioning computer-interpretable guidelines semi-automatic modeling of living guidelines: using an information extraction method. Artif. Intell. Med. **46**(1), 55–66 (2009)
7. Groot, P., Hommersom, A., Lucas, P.: Adaptation of clinical practice guidelines. Stud. Health Technol. Inform. **139**, 121–139 (2008)
8. Peleg, M.: Computer-interpretable clinical guidelines: a methodological review. J. Biomed. Inform. **46**(4), 744–763 (2013)
9. Antoniou, G., Van Harmelen, F.: Web ontology language: OWL. In: Staab, S., Studer, R. (eds.) Handbook on Ontologies, pp. 67–92. Springer, Heidelberg (2004)
10. Harris, S., Seaborne, A., Prud hommeaux, E.: SPARQL 1.1 query language. W3C Recommendation 21 (2013)
11. Flouris, G., Huang, Z., Pan, J.Z., Plexousakis, D., Wache, H.: Inconsistencies, negations and changes in ontologies. In: Proceedings of the National Conference on Artificial Intelligence, vol. 21, p. 1295. AAAI Press, MIT Press, Menlo Park, Cambridge (2006)
12. Wang, D., Peleg, M., Tu, S.W., Boxwala, A.A., Greenes, R.A., Patel, V.L., Shortliffe, E.H.: Representation primitives, process models and patient data in computer-interpretable clinical practice guidelines: a literature review of guideline representation models. Int. J. Med. Inform. **68**(1), 59–70 (2002)
13. Latoszek-Berendsen, A., Tange, H., Van Den Herik, H., Hasman, A.: From clinical practice guidelines to computer-interpretable guidelines. Methods Inform. Med. **49**(6), 550–570 (2010)
14. De Clercq, P., Kaiser, K., Hasman, A.: Computer-interpretable guideline formalisms. Stud. Health Technol. Inform. **139**, 22 (2008)
15. Peleg, M., Tu, S., Bury, J., Ciccarese, P., Fox, J., Greenes, R.A., Hall, R., Johnson, P.D., Jones, N., Kumar, A., et al.: Comparing computer-interpretable guideline models: a case-study approach. J. Am. Med. Inform. Assoc. **10**(1), 52–68 (2003)

16. Boxwala, A.A., Peleg, M., Tu, S., Ogunyemi, O., Zeng, Q.T., Wang, D., Patel, V.L., Greenes, R.A., Shortliffe, E.H.: GLIF3: a representation format for sharable computer-interpretable clinical practice guidelines. J. Biomed. Inform. **37**(3), 147–161 (2004)

17. Sutton, D.R., Taylor, P., Earle, K.: Evaluation of PROforma as a language for implementing medical guidelines in a practical context. BMC Med. Inform. Decis. Mak. **6**(1), 20 (2006)

18. Miksch, S., Shahar, Y., Johnson, P.: Asbru: a task-specific, intention-based, and time-oriented language for representing skeletal plans. In: Proceedings of the 7th Workshop on Knowledge Engineering: Methods & Languages (KEML 1997), pp. 9–19. The Open University, Milton Keynes, UK (1997)

19. Shalom, E., Shahar, Y., Lunenfeld, E.: An architecture for a continuous, user-driven, and data-driven application of clinical guidelines and its evaluation. J. Biomed. Inform. **59**, 130–148 (2016)

20. Isern, D., Moreno, A.: Computer-based execution of clinical guidelines: a review. Int. J. Med. Inform. **77**(12), 787–808 (2008)

21. Galopin, A., Bouaud, J., Pereira, S., Séroussi, B.: Using an ontological modeling to evaluate the consistency of clinical practice guidelines: application to the comparison of three guidelines on the management of adult hypertension. In: MIE, pp. 38–42 (2014)

22. Pérez, B., Porres, I.: Authoring and verification of clinical guidelines: a model driven approach. J. Biomed. Inform. **43**(4), 520–536 (2010)

23. Domínguez, E., Pérez, B., Zapata, M.: Towards a traceable clinical guidelines application. Methods Inf. Med. **49**(6), 571–580 (2010)

24. Shiffman, R.N., Michel, G., Rosenfeld, R.M., Davidson, C.: Building better guidelines with bridge-wiz: development and evaluation of a software assistant to promote clarity, transparency, and implementability. J. Am. Med. Inform. Assoc. **19**(1), 94–101 (2012)

25. Trivedi, M., Kern, J., Marcee, A., Grannemann, B., Kleiber, B., Bettinger, T., Altshuler, K., McClelland, A., et al.: Development and implementation of computerized clinical guidelines: barriers and solutions. Methods Inf. Med. **41**(5), 435–442 (2002)

26. Jafarpour, B., Abidi, S.R., Abidi, S.S.R.: Exploiting semantic web technologies to develop OWL-based clinical practice guideline execution engines. J. Biomed. Health Inform. **20**(1), 388–398 (2014)

27. Casteleiro, M.A., Des Diz, J.J.: Clinical practice guidelines: a case study of combining OWL-S, OWL, and SWRL. Knowl.-Based Syst. **21**(3), 247–255 (2008)

28. Mancia, G., Fagard, R., Narkiewicz, K., Redán, J., Zanchetti, A., Böhm, M., Christiaens, T., Cifkova, R., De Backer, G., Dominiczak, A., et al.: 2013 practice guidelines for the management of arterial hypertension of the european society of hypertension (ESH) and the european society of cardiology (ESC): ESH/ESC task force for the Management of Arterial Hypertension. J. Hypertens. **31**(10), 1925–1938 (2013)

29. James, P., Oparil, S., Carter, B., et al.: 2014 evidence-based guideline for the management of high blood pressure in adults: Report from the panel members appointed to the eighth joint national committee (JNC 8). JAMA **311**(5), 507–520 (2014). http://dx.doi.org/10.1001/jama.2013.284427

30. Oliveira, T., Novais, P., Neves, J.: Development and implementation of clinical guidelines: an artificial intelligence perspective. Artif. Intell. Rev. **42**(4), 999–1027 (2014)

31. Riano, D.: The SDA* model: a set theory approach. In: Twentieth IEEE International Symposium on Computer-Based Medical Systems (CBMS 2007), pp. 563–568. IEEE (2007)
32. Meditskos, G., Dasiopoulou, S., Efstathiou, V., Kompatsiaris, I.: SP-ACT: a hybrid framework for complex activity recognition combining OWL and SPARQL rules. In: IEEE International Conference on Pervasive Computing and Communications Workshops (PERCOM Workshops), pp. 25–30. IEEE (2013)

Comorbidity and Clinical Process Management

Generating Conflict-Free Treatments
for Patients with Comorbidity
Using Answer Set Programming

Elie Merhej[1], Steven Schockaert[2](✉), T. Greg McKelvey[4](✉),
and Martine De Cock[1,3](✉)

[1] Ghent University, Ghent, Belgium
{elie.merhej,martine.decock}@ugent.be
[2] Cardiff University, Cardiff, UK
schockaerts1@cardiff.ac.uk
[3] University of Washington Tacoma, Tacoma, USA
mdecock@u.washington.edu
[4] KenSci, Seattle, USA
Greg@KenSci.com

Abstract. Conflicts in recommended medical interventions regularly
arise when multiple treatments are simultaneously needed for patients
with comorbid diseases. An approach that can automatically repair such
inconsistencies and generate conflict-free combined treatments is thus
a valuable aid for clinicians. In this paper we propose an answer set
programming based method that detects and repairs conflicts between
treatments. The answer sets of the program directly correspond to proposed treatments, accounting for multiple possible solutions if they exist.
We also include the possibility to take preferences based on drug-drug
interactions into account while solving inconsistencies. We show in a case
study that our method results in more preferred treatments than standard approaches.

1 Introduction

Clinical Practice Guidelines (CPGs) are documents created by experts in the
medical field in order to help clinicians in treating certain diseases [10]. To make
CPGs more accessible and easier to use, many frameworks have been developed
that gather important information from a relevant CPG and transform it into
a computer interpretable format [2,7,12]. The resulting representation is called
a Computer Interpretable Guideline (CIG). These frameworks usually create
task networks that represent possible treatments of the disease based on certain
actions, decisions and tests. When a physician wants to treat a specific disease,
they consult the corresponding task network and follow the presented procedure

---

T.G. McKelvey—University of Washington Occupational and Environmental
Medicine Fellow.

D. Riaño et al. (Eds.): KR4HC/ProHealth 2016, LNAI 10096, pp. 111–119, 2017.
DOI: 10.1007/978-3-319-55014-5_7

based on the test results that are available for the patient. A lot of research has been done to improve CIGs by including, for example, patient-specific information in the generated task networks [11,13], different kinds of treatments [1] and even rules about hospital and insurance policies in order to create the best possible personalized treatment for every patient. In addition, research has been done for the verification of the resulting medical guidelines [4].

It is important, however, to note that CPGs were originally designed to treat every disease separately. Recent studies have shown that the number of patients with comorbidity, i.e. diagnosed with multiple diseases simultaneously, keeps rising [6]. Combining CIGs for individual diseases regularly results in conflicts between the recommended treatments. These conflicts can be on different levels: drug-drug interactions, drug-disease interactions, etc. Often these conflicts can be solved by the expertise of the physician, especially when swapping a drug by another one could resolve the conflict. Given the increasing number of CIGs and the complexity of the presented treatments, a system that can automatically detect [15] and repair inconsistencies when combining multiple CIGs [5,9] would be a valuable aid for clinicians.

Building on recent work by Wilk et al. [14], implemented in Zhang and Zhang [16], we present in this paper an answer set programming (ASP) based approach for generating conflict-free treatments for comorbid patients. ASP is a declarative problem solving language, which allows one to describe a problem as a set of logical rules. ASP solvers are then used to find answer sets, i.e. the sets of facts that satisfy all the encoded rules. In our case, the ASP rules represent the method to detect and repair conflicts in candidate treatments, while the answer sets correspond to valid combined treatments. Removing inconsistencies in treatments involves applying mitigation operators (MOs) [14]. These operators act like functions that take as input one point of contention (i.e. conflict) introduced by a specific pair of treatments, and provide as output a set of modifications to be applied on one or both treatments to eliminated the point of contention. In other words, an MO may suggest removing a specific drug from a treatment, substituting a drug by an alternative one, or even performing a new action in a treatment to avoid a particular conflict. However, while MOs focus on eliminating one specific conflict, they can sometimes introduce undesirable drug-drug interactions to combined treatments. Therefore, we define preferences among the answer sets by assigning a penalty based on the drug-drug interactions they contain. This penalty is equal to the sum of individual penalties introduced by every drug-drug interaction found, which depends on the severity of the corresponding interaction. Treatment penalties induce a ranking from the most preferred valid treatment (i.e. with the smallest penalty) to the least preferred (i.e. with the highest penalty). The main differences between our approach and the work by Zhang and Zhang [16] are:

- All the answer sets that we generate are valid solution treatments.
- We apply one MO at a time, instead of all simultaneously, until a point of contention is eliminated.

– We introduce preferences among solution treatments based on drug-drug interactions, to select the most desirable treatment among the given candidates.

The remainder of the paper is structured as follows: after recalling some pre-
liminaries about ASP in Sect. 2, in Sect. 3 we present a method to resolve conflicts
that arise when applying multiple CPGs on a patient with comorbid diseases,
and rank solution treatments based on drug-drug interactions. In Sect. 4, we
show the advantages of our approach by introducing a case study that involves
the task networks from the CPGs for duodenal ulcer (DU) and transient ischemic
attack (TIA). Finally, we conclude in Sect. 5.

2   Answer Set Programming

Answer Set Programming (ASP) is a declarative problem solving language [8],
which allows one to describe a problem as a set of rules of the form

$$h \leftarrow a_1, \ldots, a_j, not\ b_{j+1}, \ldots, not\ b_k \tag{1}$$

ASP solvers can then find the answer sets (see below) which correspond to the
solutions of the encoded problem. Let r be an ASP rule of the form (1). The head
and the body of r are respectively defined as $head(r) = h$ and $body(r) = \{a_1, \ldots,$
$a_j, not\ b_{j+1}, \ldots, not\ b_k\}$. The "," in the body of r represents a conjunction. If
$body(r) = \emptyset$, then r is called a *fact*. If $head(r) = \emptyset$, then r is called a *constraint*.
Constraints act as filters on the possible answer sets. The keyword *not* represents
negation-as-failure in ASP, where *not a* intuitively holds whenever we cannot
derive that a holds. Let $body^+(r) = \{a_1, \ldots, a_j\}$ and $body^-(r) = \{b_{j+1}, \ldots, b_k\}$.
A set of atoms X is closed under Π if for any rule $r \in \Pi$, $head(r) \in X$ whenever
$body^+(r) \subseteq X$. The smallest set of atoms closed under Π is denoted by $Cn(\Pi)$.
The reduct Π^X of Π relative to X is defined by $\Pi^X = \{head(r) \leftarrow body^+(r) \mid r \in$
Π and $body^-(r) \cap X = \emptyset\}$. A set X of atoms is called an *answer set* (i.e. stable
model) of Π if $Cn(\Pi^X) = X$. For example, let Π be the answer set program
formed by the rule $c \leftarrow not\ b$, the rule $b \leftarrow not\ c$ and the fact a. This program
has two answer sets $\{a, c\}$ and $\{a, b\}$.

In practice, it is often easier to encode ASP programs using first-order rules
such as $R(X_1, X_2, X_3) \leftarrow Q(X_1, X_2), not\ S(X_3)$. Such rules should be seen as
a compact representation of a set of ASP rules, called the groundings of the
first-order rule, which are obtained by considering all possible instantiations of
the variables by constants appearing in the program. An ASP solver (e.g. *clasp*
[3]) is then used to find the answer sets of the ground program.

3   Finding Preferred Conflict-Free Treatments

As in [16], we propose an ASP implementation of the theoretical method proposed in [14] to resolve conflicts that arise in the concurrent application of CPGs
on a patient with multiple diseases. These CPGs are represented by task networks that contain their relevant information. We formulate our encoding such

that every answer set corresponds directly to a solution treatment, which is different from the encoding proposed in [16] where some answer sets correspond to invalid treatments (see Sect. 4). The facts of our ASP program encode task networks (action nodes, decision nodes, edges and labels), patient information, MOs, and a given set of points of contention that can occur[1].

To find solution treatments, we first pick a candidate treatment from the task network of every disease (rules 2 and 3). A candidate treatment corresponds to a combination of candidate edges that were selected from the task networks of the corresponding diseases. In these ASP rules, we use negation-as-failure to consider every possibility of either selecting or not selecting an edge from the network as a candidate edge. Then, we add rules to make sure that every candidate treatment, i.e. every combination of selected candidate edges, is also compliant with the encoded patient information (rules 4–6).

$$candidateEdge(Ag, X, Y) \leftarrow edge(Ag, X, Y), \ not \ nCandidateEdge(Ag, X, Y). \tag{2}$$

$$nCandidateEdge(Ag, X, Y) \leftarrow edge(Ag, X, Y), \ not \ candidateEdge(Ag, X, Y). \tag{3}$$

$$nodeInTreat(Ag, X) \leftarrow candidateEdge(Ag, X, Y). \tag{4}$$

$$nodeInTreat(Ag, Y) \leftarrow candidateEdge(Ag, X, Y). \tag{5}$$

$$\leftarrow dNode(Ag, X), \ nodeInTreat(Ag, X), \ patientInfo(X, L), \\ label(Ag, X, Y, L), \ not \ candidateEdge(Ag, X, Y). \tag{6}$$

Then, we detect active points of contention in every pair of candidate treatments by checking whether every action in a point of contention is present in the selected pair of candidate treatments. To eliminate every detected point of contention, we need to apply an applicable MO. Similar to the method of selecting candidate edges, we use negation-as-failure to consider either applying or not applying every applicable MO (rules 7 and 8). In the case where a selected MO needs to be applied, we add ASP rules that encode the instructions found in [14] to modify the candidate treatments according to the information encoded by the selected MO (rules 9–11). A solution treatment consists then of the union of these modified candidate treatments that does not contain active points of contention (rules 12–15).

$$applyMO(PocID, MoID) \leftarrow activePOC(PocID), \ applicableMO(PocID, MoID), \\ not \ napplyMO(PocID, MoID). \tag{7}$$

$$napplyMO(PocID, MoID) \leftarrow activePOC(PocID), \ applicableMO(PocID, MoID), \\ not \ applyMO(PocID, MoID). \tag{8}$$

$$solutionTreat(TD, A) \leftarrow activeAction(TD, A), \ applyMO(PocID, MoID), \\ moTD(MoID, TD), \ not \ moToBeRemoved(MoID, A). \tag{9}$$

$$solutionTreat(BD, A) \leftarrow applyMO(PocID, MoID), \ moBD(MoID, BD), \\ moRHS(MoID, pos(A)). \tag{10}$$

---

[1] For the full code, see http://www.cwi.ugent.be/ComorbidityConflictSolver.html.

$$solutionTreat(BD, A) \leftarrow activeAction(BD, A),\ applyMO(PocID, MoID),$$
$$moBD(MoID, BD),\ not\ occursIn(A, MoID). \tag{11}$$

$$solutionAction(A) \leftarrow solutionTreat(D, A). \tag{12}$$

$$ignorePOC(PocID) \leftarrow not\ solutionAction(A),\ pocAction(PocID, A). \tag{13}$$

$$pocFound(PocID) \leftarrow poc(PocID),\ not\ ignorePOC(PocID). \tag{14}$$

$$\leftarrow pocFound(PocID). \tag{15}$$

Different from [16], where all applicable MOs are applied simultaneously, we want to apply only one MO at a time to remove a point of contention. In order to do so, we add ASP rules that count the number of applied MOs for every active point of contention, and eliminate the solutions where this number is not equal to 1 (rules 16–19). Applying multiple MOs to resolve the same point of contention has a high chance of introducing multiple drugs that have the same purpose in the same treatment. This is not advised for multiple reasons. First, it creates treatments that contain a higher dosage of a substance than originally intended. Second, the number of side effects that a patient may develop increases when the number of prescribed drugs increases, and third, avoidable drug-drug interactions may be introduced.

$$appliedMOs(PocID, X) \leftarrow X = \#count\{applyMO(PocID, MoID)\},\ activePOC(PocID). \tag{16}$$

$$errorApplyingMo(PocID) \leftarrow appliedMOs(PocID, X),\ X < 1. \tag{17}$$

$$errorApplyingMo(PocID) \leftarrow appliedMOs(PocID, X),\ X > 1. \tag{18}$$

$$\leftarrow errorApplyingMo(PocID). \tag{19}$$

Among all solution treatments found by the rules above, some might be preferred over others depending on the severity of drug-drug interactions that are introduced to the treatment after applying the corresponding MO. These interactions may persist in proposed valid solution treatments due to different factors. On one hand, some drug-drug interactions may only be partially described, i.e. only the cause of the interaction is known, but the way to mitigate it is still unknown. Hence, these interactions cannot be encoded in mitigation operators. We therefore propose to use them to penalize the obtained solution in case they are present. On the other hand, with the continuous improvements in clinical research, previously reliable MOs may become outdated, thus containing incomplete or inaccurate information. Applying these MOs to resolve conflicts when combining new treatments may then introduce drug-drug interactions that were previously undetected.

To induce a ranking among solution treatments, we encode in our program facts of the form "$drug(X)$" that read "X is a drug" and facts of the form "$interaction(X, Y, C)$" that read "drug X has an interaction level C with drug Y". These drug-drug interactions are included for every pair of drugs present in the treatments. Their respective interaction levels can be found in the medical literature (see Sect. 4). For every treatment we then assign a penalty that is equal to the sum of all the levels of interactions between the drugs in that treatment (rules 20–22). The treatment that minimizes this penalty is considered the best (rule 23). Note that this ASP encoding can output all possible treatments with their respective optimization value when specified by the ASP solver, and not only the best one.[2] This allows the ranking of all the treatments from most to least preferred.

$$solutionDrug(X) \leftarrow solutionAction(X), \ drug(X). \tag{20}$$

$$solutionInteraction(X, Y, C) \leftarrow interaction(X, Y, C), \ solutionDrug(X), \ solutionDrug(Y). \tag{21}$$

$$interactionsPenalty(P) \leftarrow P = \#sum[solutionInteraction(X, Y, C) = C]. \tag{22}$$

$$\#minimize[interactionsPenalty(P) = P]. \tag{23}$$

4   Case Study

We extend a use case from [16] to show the advantages of our approach. The example involves the task networks from the CPGs for duodenal ulcer (DU) and transient ischemic attack (TIA), shown in Fig. 1 [14], and a patient who is diagnosed with both diseases. The following patient information is used: H.pylori test negative, ulcer healed, hypoglyacemia absent, FAST test positive, and neurological symptoms resolved. No data is included concerning the risk of stroke. Based on this information, one candidate treatment is extracted from the task network of DU: $CT_{du}^1 = \{SA, PPI, SC\}$ and two candidate treatments from the task network of TIA: $CT_{tia}^1 = \{A, PCS\}$ and $CT_{tia}^2 = \{A, D\}$. We use the following four MOs:

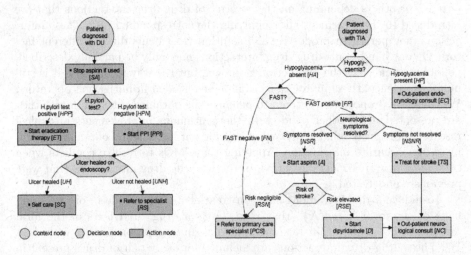

Fig. 1. Task networks for treating the DU disease (left) and the TIA disease (right).

---

[2] See http://www.cwi.ugent.be/ComorbidityConflictSolver.html.

1. MO_1: $\{tia, du, \{A, SA\}, \{pos(A)^3, neg(D)\}, \{neg(A), pos(Cl)\}, SA\}$
2. MO_2: $\{tia, du, \{A, SA\}, \{pos(A), pos(D)\}, \{pos(A), pos(D), pos(PPI)\}, SA\}$
3. MO_3: $\{tia, du, \{A, SA\}, \{pos(A), neg(D)\}, \{pos(A), pos(Cy^4)\}, SA\}$
4. MO_4: $\{tia, du, \{A, SA\}, \{pos(A), neg(D)\}, \{pos(A), pos(Fl^5)\}, SA\}$

For this scenario, our ASP rules 2–19 from Sect. 3 generate four answer sets: ST_4, ST_6, ST_7 and ST_9 shown in Table 1. One can verify that ST_4, ST_6 and ST_7 result from applying MO_3, MO_4 and MO_1 respectively to the combination of the treatments CT_{du}^1 and CT_{tia}^1. Each of these MOs correctly removes the conflict introduced by the actions "A" and "SA". Similarly, the solution treatment ST_9 arises from applying MO_2 to the combination of treatments CT_{du}^1 and CT_{tia}^2.

Table 1. Solution treatments found by Zhang's approach, and by our preference based approach. "Inv." indicates an invalid treatment. "Y" indicates that a treatment is given as a solution by the approach. "N" indicates that a treatment is not given as a solution by the approach. "Y(P)" indicates that a treatment is given as a solution by the preference based approach with the rank P.

Name	Answer set	MOs applied	Penalty	Zhang's approach	Preference based approach
ST_1	$\{PPI, SC, A, PCS, Cl, Cy, Fl\}$	MO_1, MO_3, MO_4	7	Y	N
ST_2	$\{PPI, SC, A, PCS, Cy, Fl\}$	MO_3, MO_4	4	Y	N
ST_3	$\{PPI, SC, A, PCS, Cl, Cy\}$	MO_1, MO_3	5	Y	N
ST_4	$\{PPI, SC, A, PCS, Cy\}$	MO_3	2	Y	Y (2)
ST_5	$\{PPI, SC, A, PCS, Cl, Fl\}$	MO_1, MO_4	6	Y	N
ST_6	$\{PPI, SC, A, PCS, Fl\}$	MO_4	3	Y	Y (3)
ST_7	$\{PPI, SC, PCS, Cl\}$	MO_1	3	Y	Y (3)
ST_8	$\{\}$ - Inv	Inv	Inv	Y	N
ST_9	$\{PPI, SC, A, D, NC\}$	MO_2	1	Y	Y (1)
ST_{10}	$\{\}$ - Inv	Inv	Inv	Y	N

Next, rules 20–23 can be used to induce a preference ranking over the valid solution treatments, based on the interaction levels of the drugs in the proposed treatments. We consider four levels of interactions: major, moderate, minor and no interaction, represented correspondingly in our ASP program by 3, 2, 1 and 0. These drug-drug interactions can be obtained using an interactions checker from a web database[6]. Now, running the same scenario in our ASP program identifies a preferred solution treatment: ST_9. In fact, ST_7 contains

---

[3] The keywords $pos(X)$ and $neg(X)$ refer to an action X being present and absent from a treatment respectively.

[4] Cy: Cyanocobalamin.

[5] Fl: Flibanserin.

[6] We use the "Interactions Checker" at http://www.drugs.com.

1 major drug-drug interaction between Cl and PPI (penalty $= 3$), ST_9 contains 1 minor drug-drug interaction between A and PPI (penalty $= 1$), ST_4 contains 2 minor drug-drug interactions between A and PPI, and between Cy and PPI (penalty $= 1 + 1 = 2$), and ST_6 contains 1 minor drug-drug interaction between A and PPI, and 1 moderate drug-drug interaction between Fl and PPI (penalty $= 1 + 2 = 3$). With ST_9 having the lowest penalty, it is indeed the best possible treatment (rank $= 1$).

Running the same scenario using Zhang's program [16] gives 10 answer sets, shown in Table 1. In addition to the solutions found by our preference based approach, Zhang's program gives 2 invalid solution treatments where no MOs are applied: ST_8 and ST_{10}, and 4 answer sets where multiple MOs are applied simultaneously to remove the same point of contention: ST_1, ST_2, ST_3 and ST_5. These last 4 solution treatments have penalties equal to 7, 4, 5 and 6 respectively, which are higher than penalties of solution treatments found by applying one MO at a time to solve a specific point of contention. This shows that applying multiple MOs concurrently may introduce avoidable and potentially more dangerous drug-drug interactions.

5   Conclusion

The number of patients diagnosed with multiple diseases is rising. In this preliminary paper, we presented an extension of Zhang and Zhang's ASP encoding for the problem of generating conflict-free treatments for patients with comorbidity [16]. A noteworthy difference between our approach and the work in [16] is that all answer sets of our ASP program directly correspond to solution treatments, which makes it arguably easier to use by physicians. In addition, our ASP program adheres closer to [14] in applying one MO at a time instead of all simultaneously, in the case where multiple applicable MOs are available. This distinction is clinically important because applying multiple MOs in parallel has a high chance of introducing multiple drugs that have the same purpose in the same treatment. Furthermore, we refined our ASP program with a ranking mechanism based on the severity of drug-drug interactions in solution treatments, thereby providing a technique to identify preferred treatments. An interesting direction for future research involves expanding the current ASP encoding with multiple ways of defining preferences between treatments, such as different types of interactions (drug-disease, drug-food, etc.) to complement the drug-drug interactions that we already included. We also plan to work with multiple medical experts in order to create a better encoding of the candidate treatments specified in clinical guidelines that accounts for the time variable, and more specific action nodes.

References

1. Barr, J., Fraser, G.L., Puntillo, K., Ely, E.W., Gélinas, C., Dasta, J.F., Davidson, J.E., Devlin, J.W., Kress, J.P., Joffe, A.M., et al.: Clinical practice guidelines for the management of pain, agitation, and delirium in adult patients in the intensive care unit. Crit. Care Med. **41**(1), 263–306 (2013)

2. De Clercq, P.A., Blom, J.A., Korsten, H.H., Hasman, A.: Approaches for creating computer-interpretable guidelines that facilitate decision support. Artif. Intell. Med. **31**(1), 1–27 (2004)
3. Gebser, M., Kaufmann, B., Neumann, A., Schaub, T.: *clasp*: a conflict-driven answer set solver. In: Baral, C., Brewka, G., Schlipf, J. (eds.) LPNMR 2007. LNCS (LNAI), vol. 4483, pp. 260–265. Springer, Heidelberg (2007). doi:10.1007/978-3-540-72200-7_23
4. Hommersom, A., Groot, P., Lucas, P.J., Balser, M., Schmitt, J.: Verification of medical guidelines using background knowledge in task networks. IEEE Trans. Knowl. Data Eng. **19**(6), 832–846 (2007)
5. Jafarpour, B., Abidi, S.S.R.: Merging disease-specific clinical guidelines to handle comorbidities in a clinical decision support setting. In: Peek, N., Marín Morales, R., Peleg, M. (eds.) AIME 2013. LNCS (LNAI), vol. 7885, pp. 28–32. Springer, Heidelberg (2013). doi:10.1007/978-3-642-38326-7_5
6. Jakovljevic, M., Ostojic, L.: Comorbidity and multimorbidity in medicine today: challenges and opportunities for bringing separated branches of medicine closer to each other. Psychiatr. Danub. **25**(Suppl 1), 18–28 (2013)
7. Latoszek-Berendsen, A., Tange, H., Van Den Herik, H., Hasman, A., et al.: From clinical practice guidelines to computer-interpretable guidelines. Methods Inf. Med. **49**(6), 550–570 (2010)
8. Lifschitz, V.: What is answer set programming? In: AAAI, vol. 8, pp. 1594–1597 (2008)
9. López-Vallverdú, J.A., Riaño, D., Collado, A.: Rule-based combination of comorbid treatments for chronic diseases applied to hypertension, diabetes mellitus and heart failure. In: Lenz, R., Miksch, S., Peleg, M., Reichert, M., Riaño, D., Teije, A. (eds.) KR4HC/ProHealth-2012. LNCS (LNAI), vol. 7738, pp. 30–41. Springer, Heidelberg (2013). doi:10.1007/978-3-642-36438-9_2
10. Panel, D.: Clinical practice guidelines, vol. I. Agency for Health Care Policy and Research, Washington, DC (1993)
11. Spiotta, M., Bottrighi, A., Giordano, L., Theseider Dupré, D.: Conformance analysis of the execution of clinical guidelines with basic medical knowledge and clinical terminology. In: Miksch, S., Riaño, D., Teije, A. (eds.) KR4HC 2014. LNCS (LNAI), vol. 8903, pp. 62–77. Springer, Cham (2014). doi:10.1007/978-3-319-13281-5_5
12. Ten Teije, A., Miksch, S., Lucas, P.: Computer-Based Medical Guidelines and Protocols: A Primer and Current Trends, vol. 139. Ios Press, Amsterdam (2008)
13. Tu, S.W., Campbell, J.R., Glasgow, J., Nyman, M.A., McClure, R., McClay, J., Parker, C., Hrabak, K.M., Berg, D., Weida, T., et al.: The sage guideline model: achievements and overview. J. Am. Med. Inf. Assoc. **14**(5), 589–598 (2007)
14. Wilk, S., Michalowski, W., Michalowski, M., Farion, K., Hing, M.M., Mohapatra, S.: Mitigation of adverse interactions in pairs of clinical practice guidelines using constraint logic programming. J. Biomed. Inf. **46**(2), 341–353 (2013)
15. Zamborlini, V., Hoekstra, R., Da Silveira, M., Pruski, C., ten Teije, A., van Harmelen, F.: Inferring recommendation interactions in clinical guidelines. Semant. Web **7**(4), 421–446 (2016)
16. Zhang, Y., Zhang, Z.: Preliminary result on finding treatments for patients with comorbidity. In: Miksch, S., Riaño, D., Teije, A. (eds.) KR4HC 2014. LNCS (LNAI), vol. 8903, pp. 14–28. Springer, Cham (2014). doi:10.1007/978-3-319-13281-5_2

Detecting New Evidences for Evidence-Based Medical Guidelines with Journal Filtering

Qing Hu[1,2]([✉]), Zhisheng Huang[1], Annette ten Teije[1], and Frank van Harmelen[1]

[1] Department of Computer Science, VU University Amsterdam,
Amsterdam, The Netherlands
{qhu400,huang,annette,Frank.van.Harmelen}@cs.vu.nl
[2] College of Computer Science and Technology,
Wuhan University of Science and Technology, Wuhan, China

Abstract. Evidence-based medical guidelines are systematically developed recommendations with the aim to assist practitioner and patients decisions regarding appropriate health care for specific clinical circumstances, and are based on evidence described in medical research papers. Evidence-based medical guidelines should be regularly updated, such that they can serve medical practice using based on the latest medical research evidence. A usual approach to detecting new evidences is to use a set of terms which appear in a guideline conclusion or recommendation and create queries over a bio-medical search engine such as PubMed with a ranking over a selected subset of terms to search for relevant new research papers. However, the sizes of the found relevant papers are usually very large (i.e. over a few hundreds, even thousands), which results in a low precision of the search. This makes it for medical professionals quite difficult to find which papers are really interesting and useful for updating the guideline. We propose a filtering step to decrease the number of papers. More exactly we are interested in the question if we can reduce the number of papers with no or a slightly lower recall. A plausible approach is to introduce journal filtering, such that evidence appear in those top journals are preferred.

In this paper, we extend our approach of detecting new papers for updating evidence-based medical guideline with a journal filtering step. We report our experiments and show that (1) the method with journal filtering can indeed gain a large reduction of the number of papers (69.73%) with a slightly lower recall (14.29%); (2) we show that the journal filtering method keeps relatively more high level evidence papers (category A) and removes all the low level evidence papers (category D).

1 Introduction

In evidence-based medical guidelines are the recommendations and conclusions supported by the best available evidence. Usually, the evidences in guidelines come from the scientific medical publications. Through evidence-based medical guidelines, the clinical practitioners can easily find supporting medical knowledge and quickly make decision for diagnosis, treatment, and follow-up.

D. Riaño et al. (Eds.): KR4HC/ProHealth 2016, LNAI 10096, pp. 120–132, 2017.
DOI: 10.1007/978-3-319-55014-5_8

In an ideal scenario, a guideline is expected to be updated immediately after new relevant evidence is published, so that the updated guideline can serve medical practice using latest medical research evidence. However, the update of the guideline is often lagging behind medical scientific publications. Because of the sheer volume of medical publications, that is not easy to be achieved. Not only are the number of medical articles and the size of medical information very large, but also they are updated very frequently. For example, PubMed[1], a bibliographic database of citations and abstracts, are about 21,721 citations on breast cancer for biomedical literature from MEDLINE[2] in year 2015. That means on average there appear roughly 60 new papers on breast cancer in a single day. For medical professionals and guideline designers it is rather impossible to make an exhaustive search over the publications in their concerned topic.

A natural solution to solve that problem is to use information retrieval or machine learning technology to find relevant new evidence automatically. Reinders et al. [12] describe a system to find relevant new evidence for guideline updates. The approach is based on MeSH terms and their TF-IDF weights. That results in the problem that the number of returned relevant articles is sometimes too large (sometimes over a few million). Iruetaguena et al. [8] also develop an approach to finding new evidences. That method is also based on gathering all relevant articles by searching the PubMed website, and then uses the Rosenfeld-Shiffman filtering algorithm to select the relevant articles. The experiment of that approach shows the recall is excellent, but the precision is very low (10.000 articles contain only 7 goal articles) [12]. In [4], we propose a method that uses a semantic distance measure to automatically find relevant new evidence to support guideline updates. The advantage of using semantic distance is that the relevance measure can be achieved via the co-occurrence of terms in a bio-medical article, which can be easily obtained via a bio-medical search engine such as PubMed, instead of gathering a large corpus for the analysis.

In the existing approaches, the sizes of found papers (evidence) are usually large. This makes it for medical professionals very difficult to find which papers are really interesting and useful. In our previous work, we have implemented a guideline update tool, which covers various approaches of medical guideline update [5]. The tool was evaluated by three medical experts and the evaluation medical experts also mentioned there were still too many irrelevant articles suggested as evidence in the results. In order to improve the precision of search results the solutions are reducing the sizes of the search results or introducing ranking strategies. The guideline designers or other medical professionals can then focus on those papers that are really relevant. An approach is to consider the provenance information in the search and the ranking. Namely we consider the sources and originality of found evidence in the search. One of the provenance approaches is to consider the papers which appear in the top journal only and ignore those papers which appear in other journals. We call this approach *journal filtering*. However, note that the approach of journal filtering would not improve

---

[1] http://www.ncbi.nlm.nih.gov/pubmed.

[2] http://www.nlm.nih.gov/bsd/pmresources.html.

the recall of the searches. An interesting research question here is: whether or not we can use a slightly lower recall to gain a much higher precision for a trade-off between the recall and the precision. We use the number of papers as proxy for the precision. In this paper, we will explore how the approach of journal filtering can improve the precision of the search results in detecting new evidence for update of evidence-based medical guidelines. We report our experiments with the proposed approach and show that this new approach can indeed achieve the goal of obtaining a much higher precision (reduction of number of relevant papers) with a slightly lower recall in the search. Furthermore we investigate the journal filtering behaviour with respect to the level of evidence of the papers.

The rest of this paper is organized as follows: Sect. 2 presents the basic structure of guidelines and the procedure of guideline update and present the existing approaches for finding new and relevant evidence for guidelines. Section 3 proposes the journal filtering approach. Section 4 discusses the experiments of our filtering method on the update of guidelines. Section 5 discusses future work and concludes.

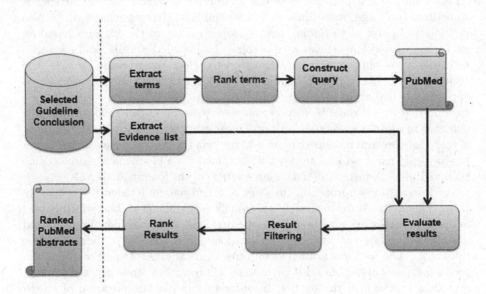

Fig. 1. Workflow of journal filtering approach

2   Evidence-Based Guidelines and Guideline Updates

Evidence-based medical guidelines are based on published scientific research findings. Those findings are usually found in medical publications such as those in PubMed. Selected articles are evaluated by an expert for their research quality, and are graded for the degree to which they contribute evidence using a classification system [11]. A classification on medical evidence is proposed in [10,11],

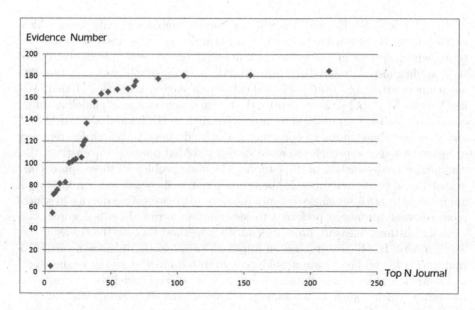

Fig. 2. The numbers of evidences which appear in the top N oncological journals

which consists of the five evidence-classes: Type A1: Systematic reviews, or that comprise at least several A2 quality trials whose results are consistent; Type A2: High-quality randomized comparative clinical trials with sufficient size and consistency; Type B: Randomized clinical trials of moderate quality or insufficient size, or other comparative trials (non-randomized, comparative cohort study, patient control study); Type C: Non-comparative trials, and Type D: Opinions of experts.

Based on this classification of evidence, a guideline conclusion/recommendation (sometimes called *guideline items*) are annotated with an evidence level. In [10], the following four evidence levels on guideline items, are proposed: Level 1: Based on 1 systematic review (type A1) or at least 2 independent A2 reviews; Level 2: Based on at least 2 independent type B reviews; Level 3: Based on 1 type A2 or B research, or any level of C research, and Level 4: Opinions of experts.

Here is an example of a conclusion in a guideline in [10]:

```
Classification: Level 1
Conclusion:    The diagnostic reliability of ultrasound with
               an uncomplicated cyst is very high.
Evidence:      A1 Kerlikowske 2003
               B Boerner 1999, Thurfjell 2002, Vargas 2004
```

which consists of a conclusion classification 'Level 1', a guideline statement, and its evidence items with one item classified as A1 and three items classified as B (jointly justifying the Level 1 of this conclusion).

In order to check if there is any new evidence from a scientific paper which is relevant to the guideline statement, a natural way to proceed is to use the terms which appear in the guideline statement (in the example above: terms such as 'diagnostic', 'reliability', 'ultrasound', and 'uncomplicated cyst') to create a query to search over a biomedical search engine such as PubMed. We use Xerox's NLP tool [1,2] to identify the terms which appear in guideline statements from well-known medical terminologies such as UMLS and SNOMED CT, and then use these terms to construct a PubMed query to search for relevant evidence. A naive approach to create such a PubMed query is to construct the conjunction or disjunction of those terms. The main problem of those approaches is that the semantic relevance of the terms is not well considered. An improved approach is to use a semantic distance measure to create search queries in which more relevant terms are preferred to less relevant terms. In other words, the semantic distance measure provides us with a method to rank the terms in the search query. In [4], we propose an approach of semantic distance measure to rank terms for finding relevant evidences from bio-medical search engine such as PubMed. The semantic distance measure is developed based co-occurrence of two terms which appear in the same publication with the assumption that: the more frequently two terms co-occurrence at the same paper, the more semantically related they are. Those co-occurrence data can be easily obtained from PubMed.

3   Finding New Evidences with Journal Filtering

In the computer science, data provenance refers to the ability to trace and verify the creation of data, how it has been used or moved among different databases, as well as altered throughout its life-cycle. We search for evidence in a bio-medical search engine like PubMed. Usually those search engine can provide the corresponding provenance information about evidence. The provenance information of the evidence includes the journal names of those papers have been published and from which clinical trials those evidences are obtained. Those provenance information are considered to be useful ones to improve the quality of search, because the provenance can provide more precise information in the search and can reduce the large size of search results. An approach to do this is to consider the names of journals in the generation of the corresponding queries over PubMed. A solution is to make the selection over the found papers based on the names of selected journals. We call this approach *journal filtering*.

The workflow of journal filtering approach (Fig. 1) can be considered by adding the filtering process step into the usual workflow for detecting new and relevant papers for evidence-based medical guidelines. The workflow consists of several main steps that need to be executed.

The steps are as follows:

- Select a guideline statement (conclusion) for detecting its new and relevant papers (evidence).
- Extract the terms that appear in the selected guideline statement by using Xerox's NLP tool Xmedlan (which is supported by medical terminologies/ontologies, such as UMLS and SNOMED CT).
- Rank the terms with a semantic relevance measure. We use the Normalized PubMed Distance (NPD) for the ranking over terms.
- Construct PubMed queries based on ranked terms and obtain the results of the PubMed queries.
- Obtain the PMIDs (PMID is the PubMed Unique Identifier for each paper) of the evidences by executing the semantic queries (i.e., SPARQL queries) over a SPARQL endpoint which stores the semantic representation of the evidence-based medical guidelines [7]. In our implementation, we use the LarKC platform [3] as the triple store.
- Evaluate the results by using the heuristic function which is developed based on the criteria of the coverage of original evidences, the coverage of selected terms, and the size of the returned results, to find most-satisfying result.
- Select partial results by journal filtering to reduce the size of the found results.
- Rank the results by their evidence levels.
- Present the final results to the users.

Table 1. The results of non-journal filtering approach

| ID | Goal paper number | Non-journal filtering | | |
		Found goal paper	Found paper	Found goal paper %
04_1_1	5	2	73	40%
04_1_2	2	1	69	50%
04_1_3	4	4	300	100%
04_3_1	14	2	278	14.29%
04_3_2	2	2	78	100%
04_3_3	2	0	300	0%
04_3_5	2	2	72	100%
04_3_6	8	1	69	12.5%
04_3_7	2	0	119	0%
04_4_1	5	0	300	0%
04_4_2	6	3	290	50%
04_5_1	3	0	52	0%
04_6_1	5	2	82	40%
04_6_2	3	1	100	33.33%
04_7_1	2	1	300	50%
04_8_1	2	0	300	0%
Total	67	21	2782	
Average	4.19	1.31	173.88	

4   Experiment and Results

We have conducted several experiments on the journal-filtering approach for finding relevant papers of guideline update. We redo the experiments from [5], and compare the results with the same method including the journal-filtering.

Similarly we use the Dutch breast cancer guideline (version 1.0, 2004) and the Dutch breast cancer guideline (version 2.0, 2012) as the test data. We select several guideline conclusions in the Dutch breast cancer version 1.0 to find relevant papers and test whether or not the system can find those papers which have been used in the Dutch breast cancer guideline version 2.0 (i.e., "goal" paper), like that we have reported in [4,5]. Moreover, we will compare the results of the journal filtering approach with the results of non-filtering approach to see whether we are filtering in the right way: reducing the number of papers while keeping the "goal" papers, or slightly lower the recall. In order to test the proposed approach, we select sixteen guideline conclusions in the Dutch breast cancer guideline version 1.0, which can also find the corresponding guideline conclusions in the second version.

Table 2. The results of journal filtering approach

| ID | Goal paper number | Journal filtering | | | |
		Found goal paper	Found paper	Found goal paper%	Reduced %
04_1_1	5	2	23	40%	68.49%
04_1_2	2	1	29	50%	57.97%
04_1_3	4	3	112	75%	62.67%
04_3_1	14	2	129	14.29%	53.60%
04_3_2	2	2	22	100%	71.79%
04_3_3	2	0	127	0%	57.67%
04_3_5	2	2	20	100%	72.22%
04_3_6	8	1	20	12.5%	71.01%
04_3_7	2	0	38	0%	68.07%
04_4_1	5	0	123	0%	59.00%
04_4_2	6	3	113	50%	61.03%
04_5_1	3	0	6	0%	88.46%
04_6_1	5	1	7	20%	91.46%
04_6_2	3	1	15	33.33%	85.00%
04_7_1	2	0	38	0%	87.33%
04_8_1	2	0	20	0%	93.33%
Total	67	18	842		
Average	4.19	1.13	52.63		
Difference%		14.29	69.73		

Table 3. The results with evidence classes by non-journal filtering

ID	Non-journal filtering						
	A1	A2	B	C	D	Unknown	Total
04_1_1	3	15	25	22	0	8	73
04_1_2	1	7	24	26	0	11	69
04_1_3	12	71	91	63	0	63	300
04_3_1	10	41	72	130	0	25	278
04_3_2	1	7	29	25	0	16	78
04_3_3	7	18	91	112	2	70	300
04_3_5	2	9	27	24	0	10	72
04_3_6	2	3	21	34	1	8	69
04_3_7	3	4	43	50	0	19	119
04_4_1	23	27	87	94	1	68	300
04_4_2	14	46	101	96	0	33	290
04_5_1	0	4	22	17	0	9	52
04_6_1	0	0	28	35	2	17	82
04_6_2	1	2	29	47	0	21	100
04_7_1	2	5	102	68	0	123	300
04_8_1	10	4	88	43	2	153	300
Total	91	263	880	886	8	654	2782
Average	5.69	16.44	55	55.38	0.50	40.88	173.88

Journal Filtering. For the journal filtering, we select the oncology journals which are ranked by SJR (SCImago Journal and Country Rank http://www.scimagojr.com/). There are 320 journals that have been ranked. There are several interesting questions about the relationship between selected journals and used evidences in medical guidelines:

- Are those papers (evidence) used in existing guidelines always published in the top journals?
- How many top journals should be selected for journal filtering with a reasonably good coverage?
- How much reduction on the number of papers can be gained by which loss of recall?

In order to ask those questions above, we make an analysis on the papers which have been used in those two versions of Dutch breast cancer guidelines. Of the 311 papers used in the Dutch breast cancer guideline, we can identify 185 papers which appear in an oncological journal in the ranked list. The distribution of evidence which appear on the top N oncological journals is shown in Fig. 2. There appear 166 papers in the top 50 oncological journals. Namely, the top 50 oncological journal would cover 89.2% of the identified evidences. We have

Table 4. The results with evidence classes by journal filtering

ID	Journal filtering						
	A1	A2	B	C	D	Unknown	Total
04_1_1	0	7	6	8	0	2	23
04_1_2	0	4	7	12	0	6	29
04_1_3	1	25	28	36	0	22	112
04_3_1	5	19	28	63	0	14	129
04_3_2	0	5	8	4	0	5	22
04_3_3	7	9	41	56	0	14	127
04_3_5	1	3	7	6	0	3	20
04_3_6	0	2	6	12	0	0	20
04_3_7	1	1	14	17	0	5	38
04_4_1	4	13	32	52	0	22	123
04_4_2	7	22	27	46	0	11	113
04_5_1	0	0	3	2	0	1	6
04_6_1	0	0	2	4	0	1	7
04_6_2	0	1	3	9	0	2	15
04_7_1	1	1	13	13	0	10	38
04_8_1	1	1	7	5	0	6	20
Total	28	113	232	345	0	124	842
Average	1.75	7.06	14.50	21.56	0	7.75	52.63
Reduced%	69.23	57.03	73.64	61.06	100	81.04	69.91

observed the fact that some evidences appear in a low-ranked journal (ranked at 213). We have also found that it is not the case that all of the papers on breast cancers are published in an oncological journal. Some of papers are published on a general medical journal which is not specific to a topic. For example, the well-known medical journals such as the Lancet and New England Journal of Medicine, are not included in the list of oncological journals. We have found such 10 well-known general medical journals which cover all medical topics. Therefore, for the experiments of journal filtering on breast cancer guidelines, we select the top 50 oncological journals in the rank, plus the 10 general medical journals, which leads to 60 selected journals in total for the filtering processing.

Experiment 1: Trade-Off Between the Number of Relevant Papers and the Recall. Our first experiment is to do the journal filtering with the semantic distance approach [4] to find relevant papers for those sixteen selected guideline conclusions and use the same heuristic function to guide the search. We make a comparison between the results of journal filtering and that without journal filtering. In this experiment, we select only the first 300 evidences for the comparison if the sizes of found relevant evidences are too big (namely more than 300). The comparison results[3] are shown in Tables 1 and 2. From the tables, we can see that, the journal filtering can reduce the sizes of the found results significantly. For example, for the guideline statement 04_4_2, we obtain the 290 relevant papers without journal filtering, whereas we obtain 113 relevant ones with journal filtering. That reduces 61% of the number of papers without decreasing the recall (both can find three goal papers). In total, the journal filtering approach can reduce the size of the found results from 2,782 to 842 (which is 69,73% reduction) with the loss of found goal evidences from 21 to 18 (which is 14.29% difference). A visualization of the comparison between the sizes of found results with journal filtering and the sizes of found results without journal filtering is shown in Fig. 3. Since we are interested in whether the gain in reduction of number of papers is at the cost of decrease of recall, we could also take into account only the guideline-items that have at least 1 goal evidence. This means that we should not consider the guideline elements 04_3_3, 04_3_7, 04_4_1, 04_5_1 and 04_8_1. This gives more or less the same result of 70,05% reduction of

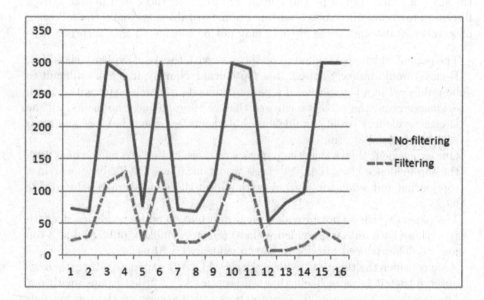

Fig. 3. Comparison between the results with journal filtering and the results without journal filtering. x-as: guideline statement row of tables (1 is 04_1_1). y-as: number of papers.

---

[3] The results of non-journal filtering in this paper are different from those in our previous ones [4,5], because they use different cutoff size and different weights on the heuristic function. In this experiment, the cutoff is 300, so that we can get less latency for the performance consideration. Furthermore, we set the weight of the coverage of original seed evidences as 0.4, and the other two weights are 0.3 and 0.3 respectively.

number of papers with a 14,29% drop in recall. An other observation is that the filter has for the majority of the conclusions only a gain in the reduction of the number of papers without recall cost: 3 out of 16 conclusions (04_1_3, 04_6_1, and 04_7_1) have a lower recall (=loss of one or more goal papers), whereas all the other cases have a reduction in number of papers without any costs of recall. Two of those three cases have a relatively high reduction rate respectively 91.46% (04_6_1) and 87.33% (04_7_1).

Experiment 2: Filtering Behaviour with Respect to the Level of Evidence of the Papers. Our second experiment is to explore how the journal filtering effects on the concrete evidence classes of the results. Namely we make a comparison with more fine-grained details on the evidence classes. We use the algorithm from [6] to identify the evidence classes of found results. In earlier studies [6] this algorithm showed on average a recall of 35% and a precision of 42%, and for A-class papers (A1+A2) the recall is 63% and the precision is 74%. This fine-grained comparison with respect to the evidence classes between the sizes of found results by the journal filtering and those by the non journal filtering are shown in Tables 3 and 4. From the tables, we have the following observations, although some of them may not be considered as a surprise:

- The papers which are claimed to be the ones with the weak evidence class (i.e., D-class) would unlikely appear in a top journal. Namely, it is more difficult to be published in a top journal if a paper claims its research result with a weak evidence. From the table we can see that of 16 guideline statements, all the D-class evidences (from 5 guideline) statements are gone (i.e., become zero) with the journal filtering.
- Our experiment shows that the papers which are claimed to be the ones with the top evidence class (i.e., A1 class) would have average likely appear in a top journal and a non-top journal (with almost the same average reduced rate 69.23%).
- The papers which do not provide a clear information on the evidence strength (i.e., those with unknown evidence class) are more unlikely published at a top journal. The reduced rate for unknown evidences is 81.04%.
- If we consider the top-class evidence level (A1+A2) papers together, then we observe that it is more likely that we keep a (A1+A2) level paper with our filter method. There are 30.27% of papers which appear on the top journals (842 evidences out of 2782 ones, 30.27%). Namely, our pre-selected 60 journals cover 30.27 percentage of the evidences in breast cancer. The selection on high level evidence papers (A1+A2) is higher namely 39.83% ((28+113)/(91+263)).
- Ideal we would like a reduction rate increasing from high-level evidence papers to low-evidence papers. The papers of the A2-class (i.e., papers based on high-quality randomized controlled trials) are more unlikely to be reduced by the journal filtering approach. From the table, we can see that the average reduced rate is 69.91%, the reduced rate on the A2 evidences is 57.03%, whereas the reduced rate on the B evidences are 73.64%. However the reduction rate on

A2 is lower than A1 (instead of higher), and the reduction rate of C (61.06%) is lower than the reduction rate of B (instead of higher).

5 Conclusion

In this paper, we have built on our approach of detecting new evidences for evidence-based medical guideline update by introducing journal filtering. From the experiments, we can see that this new approach can indeed gain a much higher precision (69.73% reduction of the number of papers) with a slightly lower recall (14.29% decrease) for detecting relevant papers. Although the journal filtering can reduce the irrelevant articles significantly from the average 174 articles into 53 articles medical professionals still think the average 53 articles for each guideline conclusion are too many. This filtering approach is a step in the right direction, but one of our future work is to continue to improve the precision of the search process, and we will perform more experiments with different guidelines, not only using Dutch breast cancer guideline. The next step is a study with guideline developers who use our tool in their guideline updating process. This will result in a real evaluation of the method in terms of precision, instead of taking only into account the number of papers.

In [9], Lewison and Sullivan present a research on how publications influence UK cancer clinical guidelines. That research finds that the geographical provenance of the publications and type of research have strong impact on selecting evidences in clinical guidelines. The UK papers were cited nearly three times as frequently as would have been expected from their presence in world oncology research. Therefore, in order to improve the precision, we can also consider the impact of geographical provenance as a feature for further filtering. We keep the filtering by geographical provenance as one of the future work. Another topic for future work is the use of GRADE[4] approach for the judgments about quality of evidence and strength of recommendations for the fine-grained comparison with respect to evidence classes (experiment 2).

Acknowledgments. This work is partially supported by the European Commission under the 7th framework programme EURECA Project, the Dutch national project COMMIT/Data2Semantics, the major international cooperation project No. 61420106005 funded by China National Foundation of Natural Science. The first author is funded by the China Scholarship Council.

References

1. Ait-Mokhtar, S., Bruijn, B.D., Hagege, C., Rupi, P.: Initial prototype for relation identification between concepts, D3.2. Technical report, EURECA Project (2013)
2. Aït-Mokhtar, S., Chanod, J.-P., Roux, C.: Robustness beyond shallowness: incremental deep parsing. Natural Lang. Eng. **8**(2), 121–144 (2002)

---

[4] www.gradeworkinggroup.org.

3. Fensel, D., van Harmelen, F., Andersson, B., Brennan, P., Cunningham, H., Della Valle, E., Fischer, F., Huang, Z., Kiryakov, A., Lee, T., School, L., Tresp, V., Wesner, S., Witbrock, M., Zhong, N., LarKC, T.: A platform for web-scale reasoning. In: Proceedings of the IEEE International Conference on Semantic Computing (ICSC 2008). IEEE Computer Society Press, CA (2008)

4. Hu, Q., Huang, Z., den Teije, A., van Harmelen, F.: Detecting new evidence for evidence-based guidelines using a semantic distance method. In: Proceedings of the 15th Conference on Artificial Intelligence in Medicine (AIME 2015) (2015)

5. Hu, Q., Huang, Z., ten Teije, A., van Harmelen, F., Marshall, M., Dekker, A.: A topic-centric approach to detecting new evidences for evidence-based medical guidelines. In: Proceedings of HEALTHINF 2016, Rome (2016)

6. Huang, Z., Hu, Q., ten Teije, A., van Harmelen, F.: Identifying evidence quality for updating evidence-based medical guidelines. In: Proceedings of International Joint Workshop KR4HC 2015 - ProHealth 2015 (2015)

7. Huang, Z., ten Teije, A., van Harmelen, F., Ait-Mokhtar, S.: Semantic representation of evidence-based clinical guidelines. In: Proceedings of 6th International Workshop on Knowledge Representation for Health Care (KR4HC 2014) (2014)

8. Iruetaguena, A., et al.: Automatic retrieval of current evidence to support update of bibliography in clinical guidelines. Expert Syst. Apps. **40**, 2081–2091 (2013)

9. Lewiaon, G., Sullivan, R.: The impact of cancer research: how publications influence uk cancer clinical guidelines. Bristish J. Cancer (2008)

10. NABON. Breast cancer, dutch guideline, version 2.0. Technical report, Integraal kankercentrum Netherland, Nationaal Borstkanker Overleg Nederland (2012)

11. NSRS. Guideline complex regional pain syndrome type i. Technical report, Netherlands Society of Rehabilitation Specialists (2006)

12. Reinders, R., ten Teije, A., Huang, Z.: Finding evidence for updates in medical guideline. In: Proceedings of HEALTHINF 2015, Lisbon (2015)

Author Index

Printed in the United States
By Bookmasters